THE

EDGE

SECOND EDITION

MODERN MANNERS FOR
BUSINESS SUCCESS

BEVERLY Y. LANGFORD

AMACOM
American Management Association
New York • Atlanta • Brussels • Chicago • Mexico City • San Francisco
Shanghai • Tokyo • Toronto • Washington, D.C

Bulk discounts available. For details visit:
www.amacombooks.org/go/specialsales
Or contact special sales:
Phone: 800-250-5thirty8
Email: specialsls@amanet.org
View all the AMACOM titles at: www.amacombooks.org
American Management Association: www.amanet.org

This publication is designed to provide accurate and authoritative information in regard to the subject matter covered. It is sold with the understanding that the publisher is not engaged in rendering legal, accounting, or other professional service. If legal advice or other expert assistance is required, the services of a competent professional person should be sought.

LIBRARY OF CONGRESS CATALOGING-IN-PUBLICATION DATA
Names: Langford, Beverly Y., author.
Title: The etiquette edge : modern manners for business success / Beverly Y.
   Langford.
Description: New York, NY : American Management Association, [2016] | Earlier
   edition: 2005.
Identifiers: LCCN 2016004846| ISBN 9780814437629 (pbk.) | ISBN
9780814437636
   (ebook)
Subjects: LCSH: Business etiquette. | Success in business.
Classification: LCC HF5389 .L36 2016 | DDC 395.5/2--dc23 LC record available
at http://lccn.loc.gov/2016004846

About AMA
American Management Association (www.amanet.org) is a world leader in talent development, advancing the skills of individuals to drive business success. Our mission is to support the goals of individuals and organizations through a complete range of products and services, including classroom and virtual seminars, webcasts, webinars, podcasts, conferences, corporate and government solutions, business books, and research. AMA's approach to improving performance combines experiential learning—learning through doing—with opportunities for ongoing professional growth at every step of one's career journey.

THE

Etiquette

EDGE

SECOND EDITION

Contents

PART 2. *Best Behaviors at Work: Interacting with Bosses and Peers*

PART 3. *Handling Sensitive Issues: Courtesy and Building Trust*

The Case for Courtesy

*T*oday's workplace is a more complex environment than it was just a couple of decades ago. Flatter organizations, decreased power distance, and increased diversity have benefited companies immensely, but with those changes have come more confusion about accepted rules of conduct and interpersonal relationships. Added to that turmoil the inescapable reach of social media and new technology that allows near-constant opportunities for creating friction with others and creating a world where we are connecting but not really connected.

Customs vary, and language and social differences can make effective interaction in the workplace, already challenging, even more daunting. The old rules don't seem to work anymore; we need new practical guidelines to avoid confusion or chaotic behavior.

Unfortunately, since the late 1900s, perhaps even beginning in the 1960s, many people have considered courtesy old-fashioned and good manners elitist. At the same time, many of us are increasingly frustrated with rudeness or social ineptness and lack of professionalism among employees, customers, coworkers, and strangers. Yet most of us will readily admit that our parents' concepts of good manners don't always work in the twenty-first century.

THE VALUE OF COURTESY TO YOUR CAREER

Many factors contribute to a person's professional success. Knowledge, skill, work ethic, integrity, ambition—all of these factors are essential to achieving our goals. However, we make a serious mistake if we ignore the importance of effective and appropriate communication and behavior, social savvy, and commonsense etiquette. Failing to recognize how one can seize a competitive advantage by leveraging good manners and courtesy in the workplace can undermine our good efforts on the job.

When asked the secret of his success, the vice president of a major technology company once answered, "It's quite simple, really. I learned to anticipate all the possibilities so that I could take action instead of merely responding. And, *I remembered the things my mother taught me*." The point he wanted to make was that these early lessons had taught him the importance of treating others well, whether we call it etiquette, good manners, courtesy, civility, or social savvy.

Without question, if you aspire to a management or leadership position, treating others with courtesy and respect is critical to building trust and credibility. And being a credible, trustworthy leader is a key factor in inspiring others to follow you. However, courtesy should not be viewed as a management tool implemented simply to manipulate others. True courtesy has as its source a genuine ability to value other people and to see their worth, regardless of their status.

Treating people courteously either out of guilt or because we feel that a particular person is important or can help our career is inauthentic, and other people will soon recognize the insincerity. On the other hand, you can learn to be genuinely courteous, and usually the effect on others and their behavior is the best reinforcement for adopting a habit of courtesy. In most cases, when we extend genuine courtesy to others, they respond positively to us. And having people respond to us positively is a great confidence booster. In turn, as we become more secure about ourselves, we become increasingly comfortable treating others well, and soon courtesy becomes an integral element of our character.

WHO CAN USE THIS BOOK?

This book provides some commonsense guidelines for handling some common workplace situations in which knowing the right behavior can make the difference in how others see us and respond to us.

Whether you are an established manager, in a new job, or entering or reentering the workforce, a quick review of how to behave in a variety of workplace situations will help you establish yourself as a socially mature, valuable colleague whom people trust, admire, and want to be around.

Interpersonal communication is always unpredictable because we are each as unique as our fingerprints. Therefore, you need to judge the ideas presented here against the requirements of your own personality and those of your audience. Choose what works for you, and put your own spin on those suggestions that work for you in order to increase the chances of making your relationships with others solid and mutually beneficial. As you read the chapters, consider how you can apply some of these principles to your current or future work situations.

GETTING THE MOST FROM THIS BOOK

Think about the interpersonal skills you want to develop. Are you uncomfortable in social situations with strangers? Do you struggle with building an effective network of contacts you can call on when you need specific resources? Do you want to make a better first impression? Do you want to increase your authority and influence among coworkers? Do working lunches give you heartburn? Are you unsure about how to interpret nonverbal signals?

Pick out the topics or chapters that seem to fit your particular needs and focus on those sections. You'll notice that each chapter ends with a bulleted summary entitled "The Bottom Line," which highlights the major messages of that section.

Although our complex world doesn't provide simple answers, we can always find ways to make interacting with our fellow human beings more rewarding and interesting. We're all on this often exciting, frustrating, perplexing, exhilarating—and rarely ever boring—journey.

If we work together, we can all enjoy the trip.

TEST YOUR CQ (COURTESY QUOTIENT)

To get started on developing courteous behaviors, take this quiz to check your courtesy quotient (CQ). The answer key at the end will give you an indication of your understanding of key issues of courtesy and interpersonal savvy and your proficiency in handling them. Some situations may depend more on good judgment than a widely-accepted rule. In case of more than one right answer, choose the one with which you would feel most comfortable. You may wish to retake the quiz after reading the book to see if you have changed your mind about any of your answers.

1. You are in the office on the telephone and another call comes in. You should:

    a) Ask the person if you can put him or her on hold.

    b) Let voicemail take it.

    c) Tell the person you are talking to that you must put him or her on hold a moment.

2. You call a colleague and put your phone on speakerphone. Another coworker is in the room. You should:

    a) Mention neither the speakerphone nor the other person in the room.

    b) Tell the person on the phone that you wish to use the speakerphone. Mention the other person in the room, and ask the person on the phone if this is okay.

    c) Tell the person on the phone that you are using the speakerphone, but don't mention the other person in the room.

3. You have exchanged a couple of angry e-mails with a coworker who, in your opinion, is being unreasonable. It's getting out of hand. You should:

    a) Stop the communication and let things cool off.

    b) Send one more blistering e-mail, summarizing the situation and how upset you are with that person's behavior, and cc the recipient's boss.

    c) Change the medium. Call the person on the telephone, or go sit down and have a face-to-face conversation.

4. You're presenting to a potential client. Suddenly this person's body language turns very negative. You should:

    a) Try to engage the person in some interaction.

    b) Stop in the middle of the presentation and ask the person what is wrong.

    c) Ask questions to determine what you said that was upsetting and attempt to rectify the situation.

    d) Ignore the situation and finish your presentation as planned.

5. You're delivering an important presentation that you don't want interrupted with questions. You should:

    a) Refuse to answer the first question that someone asks. The rest of the audience will get the message.

    b) Tell the audience beforehand that you prefer to answer all questions at the end of the presentation.

    c) Answer questions as they are asked, even though you prefer not to.

6. When communicating across language barriers, putting things in writing:

    a) Should be avoided; it can insult the international visitor's intelligence.

    b) Can be helpful; it is usually easier to read English than to hear it.

    c) Can be confusing; it is usually easier to hear English than to read it.

7. Learning to speak a few words of the language of clients, customers, or coworkers whose first language is different from yours is:

    a) Generally a good idea, as the effort communicates respect for the other culture.

    b) Generally not a good idea because they may feel patronized.

    c) Generally not a good idea, because they might be offended if you make a mistake in vocabulary or pronunciation.

8. If you meet someone whose body language is much more outgoing and expressive than yours, you should:

    a) Attempt to match it.

    b) Not attempt to match it.

9. If you meet someone whose body language is much more restrained than yours, you should:

    a) Attempt to match it.

    b) Not attempt to match it.

10. True or false: A smile is an almost universal way of communicating goodwill and cheerfulness.

11. When answering a business phone, always answer:

a) With a simple hello. It sounds more approachable and less pretentious.

b) With your name.

c) With your name, department, title, and a greeting.

12. When others are close by—for example, in an elevator or on the subway—it's okay to use your cellular telephone:

a) For any and all conversations because, after all, it's your business.

b) For lengthy conversations, so you don't get tied up at the office.

c) For short conversations of a nonsensitive or nonconfidential nature.

13. When you reach a doorway at the same time as a person of the opposite sex, the following rules apply:

a) Whoever arrives first should open the door and hold it for those who are following.

b) Men should still open doors for women.

c) Women should open doors for men to prove they are no longer oppressed.

d) Always open and hold the door for someone of either sex if that person has his or her hands full.

14. When exiting an elevator and a more senior person is toward the back, always:

a) Step aside to let that person exit first.

b) Exit first if you are closest to the door.

15. You have just heard a coworker in the cubicle next to yours speak rudely to a client on the telephone. You should:

a) Wait until the call is finished, then tell the person that the behavior is unacceptable.

b) Tell your boss.

c) Respect your coworker's privacy and refrain from commenting.

16. When having a business lunch, who pays?

a) A business lunch is always "Dutch treat."

b) You always pay for a client's lunch.

c) You never pay for a client's lunch. It's insulting.

d) Whoever invited the other person to lunch pays.

17. On a dress-down day, which of these items of clothing are generally considered inappropriate?

a) Khaki slacks.

b) Solid T-shirts.

c) Sweatpants.

d) Baseball caps.

e) Polo-type shirts.

f) Loafers without socks.

g) Thong sandals.

h) Jeans.

18. You are in a meeting with a client and several of your colleagues and you realize your boss's fly is unzipped. You should:

a) Make a joke about it and put everyone at ease.

b) Tell him immediately, even if you don't know him well.

c) Ask someone who knows him better to mention it.

19. Use social media to:

a) Let all your connections know what's going on at work.

b) Share pictures of your colleagues so that everyone gets to know each other.

c) Let everyone know exactly how you feel about people and situations.

d) Consistently present yourself in the way you want others to perceive you.

20. If you are managing a meeting and there is an adversarial relationship among the parties, try to make sure that:

    a) People sit with those with whom they agree.

    b) The seating is mixed to encourage open dialogue and discourage an adversarial environment.

ANSWERS

1. b	**6.** b	**11.** b	**16.** d
2. b	**7.** a	**12.** c	**17.** c, d, g, h
3. c	**8.** b	**13.** a, d	**18.** c
4. a, c	**9.** a	**14.** b	**19.** d
5. b	**10.** true	**15.** b	**20.** b

KEY

Number of correct responses	Your CQ
18–20	You could write this book.
15–17	You usually know how to handle yourself.
12–14	It wouldn't hurt to brush up.
Below 12	You may need to do some damage control.

PART 1

Everyday Courtesy as a Success Factor

CHAPTER 1

Manners in the Twenty-First Century

*F*inally it arrived: the new millennium. For most of us, it was full of hope and promise and fresh beginnings, but it was also filled with dire predictions and omens. Now, more than a decade later, after all the hoopla, hype, and histrionics subsided, we have passed through the gateway into a new age and have settled in to being twenty-first-century savvy. And with the traumatic and gut-wrenching events that have ushered in this new era, we may feel an ongoing urge to reflect and take stock. The picture is not all that pretty.

We see contentious dispositions and adversarial approaches to one another played out in the barrage of 24-hour news, as politicians at the highest level can no longer discuss differences civilly and issues quickly turn personal. We have become accustomed to extreme polarization and often vitriolic language and accusations from leaders and opinion makers about the people on the other side. And many of the rest of us eagerly take our cue from these politicians, celebrities, and the media. In short, rampant rudeness prevails at all levels of society—from the halls of Congress to the checkout counter to the school playground.

Are we making any progress in the civility department? Are we ruder than the generations that have gone before us, or do we still value courtesy and considerate behavior? Granted, we no longer draw and quarter people in the town square, but we gleefully pillory our fellow citizens in the media—and through social media, where cyberbullying has become an epidemic. We bemoan the rudeness of others, yet can easily justify our own actions when we are surly with a salesperson, cut off another driver on the highway (because our time is more important and we're late), or walk past coworkers without greeting them.

Indeed, our society abounds with plenty of examples of rudeness. A marketing communications manager reproached a sandwich maker at a delicatessen for ignoring her polite "thank you" at the end of her transaction. She mentioned that the proper response to "thank you" is usually "you're welcome." Rather than being embarrassed about his lack of civility, the deli employee came from behind the counter and followed the customer across the store, spewing invectives about her having the audacity to call him out on his behavior.

As a society, particularly in highly populated areas, we're touchy, brash, and easily rankled, and although we claim to value considerate behavior, we're quick to respond in kind when we experience an affront. The word "edgy" has become something of a compliment, when it used to mean that someone had consumed too much caffeine. Furthermore, we enthusiastically adopt the outrageous, the cantankerous, and the pugnacious habits of our culture's icons. In short, we spend a lot of time bemoaning the death of courtesy and not much energy trying to revive it.

THE HIGH COST OF INCIVILITY

In their 2009 book on the high cost of incivility, Christine Pearson and Christine Porath assert that incivility is damaging to businesses in a number of ways. Their study at the University of North Carolina's Kenan-Flagler School of Business highlighted as uncivil such behavior as not responding to e-mail or voice mail, habitually interrupting, backstabbing, shouting at someone, and rudeness that ultimately escalates into threatened or actual violence.

The study found that rude behavior at work is on the rise and hitting corporations where it hurts—in the balance sheet. A survey of 1,400 workers revealed that 12 percent of people who experience chronic rude behavior at work quit their jobs and 22 percent deliberately decrease their work effort. The survey found that men are seven times more likely than women to be rude at work. Rampant incivility goes far beyond political correctness or etiquette issues. Incivility makes open communication and teamwork virtually impossible.

And the situation is only getting worse. In a January 2013 *Harvard Business Review* article, Pearson and Porath showed that one-half of all employees they surveyed in 2011 reported being on the receiving end of rudeness at least once a week—compared to only one-quarter of employees surveyed in 1998. Another recent study showed that both high performers and low performers were targets for workplace bullies because they broke the boundaries of average performance.

This survey by Public Agenda, a nonpartisan opinion research organization, revealed that eight in ten Americans surveyed say a lack of respect and courtesy is not only a serious problem, but it has become worse in recent years. Respondents cited the way they are treated by business and customer service employees as inexcusable, and almost half of those surveyed have walked out of a business because of bad service.

Even more disturbing, notes the survey, is discourtesy from individuals; complaints include inconsiderate drivers, rude cell phone users, and the use of profanity. Equally troubling is the impolite and even aggressive conduct of children, which, although the survey holds parents primarily to blame, is at least in part learned from popular culture and the entertainment media.

When asked about the perceived causes of this increased rudeness, many people suggested crowding, too much anonymity, and the pressures of our high-octane lives, coupled with a declining sense of community and a general increase in selfishness and callousness.

In the workplace, the results of this phenomenon manifest themselves on the bottom line. According to a Chicago-area consulting firm specializing in corporate behavior, ignoring bad behavior in the workplace can be a costly mistake. The negative effects of workplace incivility can include the following, to name just a few:

➤ Employee-generated lawsuits
➤ Declining commitment to the organization
➤ Decreased effort
➤ Increased tardiness and absenteeism
➤ Deliberate damage to equipment and property
➤ Termination of employment to avoid dealing with instigators
➤ Poor customer service
➤ Low morale
➤ Physical violence

Just as serious as the toll on organizational effectiveness is the toll that rudeness takes on people themselves. Discourteous behavior has a negative impact on the recipient of the behavior and on the person whose behavior is impolite and disrespectful. Whether the misbehavior comes from ignorance or from a genuine combativeness, the results are the same: The person loses credibility and alienates others—damage that, once created, is difficult to reverse.

We sometimes justify rudeness because it seems to be expedient, unlike courtesy, which may seem to take too much time and effort. On the contrary, in many cases, being rude takes just as much energy as courtesy—sometimes more. For example, you will expend more force screaming at the driver who changed lanes in front of you than you will backing off a little and letting that person into your lane. Rather than becoming irate, try to empathize. Consider that perhaps the person is in unfamiliar surroundings and just realized that his or her exit is immediately ahead. On the other hand, the person may truly be an inconsiderate driver. But either way, you have more to lose by reacting rudely and angrily.

TAKING PERSONAL RESPONSIBILITY

If indeed we believe that politeness and social rituals have a civilizing effect on the population, then we all need to accept responsibility for keeping civility alive and well in the twenty-first century. Here are a few suggestions.

Consider Your Motives

Concerns about courtesy should be positively motivated. Throughout history, the advocacy of extreme manners and protocol was often a thinly veiled ploy to exclude and feel superior to others who didn't know the protocol. In fact, the words "etiquette" and "ticket" have the same etymology: the Old French *estiquet.* And, as we well know, the purpose of a ticket is to let some in and keep others out. If you encounter a rule or behavior that seems elitist, out of date, or just plain silly, use your good judgment. True courtesy benefits everyone. Its aim is not to embarrass or catch someone in a mistake.

Consider the Needs of Others

One reason we're not better at practicing civility is that it often involves putting someone else's interests ahead of our own—opening a door, stepping aside to let someone pass, turning off our cell phones during meetings. Courtesy requires a fair amount of unselfishness, a quality too often in short supply.

Indeed, one of the defining characteristics of our social structure is the constant tension between asserting individual rights and maintaining respect for others. To some of us, deferring to others seems to equate to giving up one's freedom and rights. We feel less powerful and somehow out of control when someone goes ahead of us or takes a better seat.

We find it even more difficult to maintain civility when someone is rude to us. Our natural instinct is to defend ourselves by returning the rudeness. Unfortunately, this action begins an unpleasant cycle of revenge. When we return someone else's rudeness with our own, a minor insult can escalate into a serious problem—perhaps even leading to physical violence. Our first reaction to defend ourselves and our honor ultimately makes us party to the behavior we were critical of to begin with.

Treat Others as You'd Want to Be Treated

Practically every civilization and religion has some version of this principle. Consistently applied, that simple axiom covers a lot of territory. Most people find it difficult to be rude to someone who refuses to participate in the rudeness.

Refuse to Return Rudeness

To take this approach, you have a couple of options. On the one hand, you can behave as though the incivility didn't occur, which works well for minor offenses. People find it difficult to continue unacceptable behavior if the other person responds in a way that affirms the dignity of both parties and attempts to move the encounter in a more positive direction. Or you can politely acknowledge the rudeness. If, for example, a coworker snaps at you when you request some information, you might respond with something like, "I can see that you are really busy and probably on a deadline, and I wouldn't be here if I didn't need your help."

If that approach doesn't disarm the person, you have the right to confront the rudeness courteously but more directly. For example, you might say, "You seem really upset about something. If I have offended you, I'm sorry. I'll try to get this information from someone else or speak to you later."

Only in the most extreme cases will someone continue to be rude in the face of one of these strategies. At any rate, you will be far better off if you refuse to let yourself be dragged into the fray. Furthermore, if anyone else happens to hear the exchange, you will come across as evenhanded, emotionally mature, and in control while your opponent will send all kinds of negative signals. If both of you went at it, neither would be a winner.

WHAT'S IN IT FOR YOU?

Obviously, not many people appreciate the rudeness that's rampant in our society, even though many admit that they themselves frequently fall into the pattern of discourtesy and disrespect that they abhor in others.

Not surprisingly, then, anyone who commits to becoming familiar with the right way to treat other people and who adheres to the essential tools of good manner is going to get noticed. According to Dana May Casperson, author of *Power Etiquette: What You Don't Know Can Kill Your Career*, "Good manners open doors that position and money cannot." When you are polished and professional, others perceive you as knowledgeable and confident. Conversely, if you lack polish and professionalism, people may seem willing to overlook your slipups temporarily, but they won't ignore them indefinitely. Casperson asserts that at critical points in your career, you may be passed over for someone who has learned the importance of interpersonal skills based on courtesy, knowledge, and respect for others.

THE CONSTANTLY CHANGING RULES

We'll probably never have a *Leave It to Beaver* world (did it ever really exist?), but the alternative doesn't have to be *The Jerry Springer Show*. And although the rules will continue to change as society and circumstances change—for example, the rule that a man must walk on the outside of the sidewalk to shield a woman's long, flowing skirts from being splashed by carriages on muddy streets made sense in the 19th century, but no longer applies—the principles of fair play, ethical behavior, and concern for others will always be valued. Courtesy, in the end, comes from an attitude—a sensible, enriching way of treating others, rather than merely a set of ordinances—that is a mixture of common sense and kindness.

THE BOTTOM LINE

> ➤ Incivility has become commonplace in society.
> ➤ Rudeness takes a serious toll in the workplace.
> ➤ Courtesy stems from a genuine respect for others.
> ➤ Refusing to return rudeness is an important first step toward civility.
> ➤ Courtesy can be an important competitive advantage.

CHAPTER 2

Credibility

Creating It and Keeping It

"I'll call you."
"Let's do lunch."
"We really need to get together."
"I'll get back to you later today."
"I tried to call you back, but you weren't there, and I didn't leave a message."
"I'm almost finished with that project."

*E*very day, in our personal and professional relationships, we make promises that we can't or don't intend to keep and issue statements that bear only a slight resemblance to truth. In fact, the practice of telling half-truths is so commonplace that we are barely conscious that we're doing it or that it's being done to us. We accept the fact that, whatever we call it—telling a white lie, exaggerating, or providing selective information—lying to each other in a variety of ways is an everyday part of life.

Obviously, an isolated fib here and there isn't going to hurt anything. (Do you really need to tell your best friend that her hair looks like she got caught in a ceiling fan?) But if you develop a habit of saying things you don't mean, making promises you don't keep, and misleading by cloaking reality in rhetoric, you diminish others' ability to trust you and chip away at your own credibility, which is one of your most important yet fragile assets.

Our credibility comes from a combination of who we are and what we do—a healthy balance of character and competence. It's not something anyone bestows on us; we have to earn it—and keep on earning it by what we do and say, minute by minute, day by day, and month by month. Credibility takes time to establish and, in some cases, only an instant to destroy. As the saying goes, "When you break your word, you break something that can't be mended." When people use up their credibility, it's nearly impossible to get it back. Here are some recommendations you can use to establish yourself as a credible employee, coworker, leader, and friend.

MASTERING THE ART OF STRAIGHT TALK

Although we hear a lot about *"walking* the talk," and that's certainly essential, the *talk* itself is still important. In fact, words—the language choices we make—have a huge impact on how we come across to others and how we develop a reputation for honesty and sincerity.

We can each take a significant step toward creating and maintaining our own credibility by what Pat MacMillan, CEO of Triaxia Partners, Inc., a consulting firm that specializes in team building and leadership development, calls "mastering the art of straight talk." A management consultant to top executives in a number of Fortune 500 companies, MacMillan advocates "straightforward communication that is open and honest, timely and accurate."

Straight talk doesn't always come naturally, however, and some common pitfalls can sabotage our influence and undermine our integrity. Here are a few ways to avoid the pitfalls.

Resist the temptation to stretch the truth. Dianna Booher, author of *Communicate with Confidence,* warns against developing a reputation for exaggeration. Were you on hold for fifteen minutes or was it more like five or six? Did your boss really "lose it" or merely express active concern about some aspects of your marketing plan? When your flair for the dramatic leads you to overstate, in the interest of lively conversation, you may cause people to weigh your words carefully or end up like the little boy who cried "wolf" until no one believed him.

If you earn a dubious reputation for hyperbole, you'll find that when you actually deliver unembellished information, people will mentally subtract a few degrees from anything you tell them, convinced that you are inflating the facts as usual. In the workplace, your tendency to amplify a story may affect how colleagues perceive you, which damages your effectiveness. An urgent situation with a key client, for example, may not get the reaction and attention it deserves from your colleagues or your manager, or your explanation why a particular project is delayed may be seen as a creative excuse rather than a legitimate reason.

Avoid excessively using jargon and buzzwords. In a jargon-filled world, a stock market crash becomes an "unplanned equity retreat"; companies don't fire people but go through "workforce adjustments" and "headcount reductions"; and taxes are "revenue enhancements." We seem surrounded by those who, as Voltaire once said, use words to hide their thoughts. Is this a harmless tactic? Not really. The practice calls intentions into question. It pretends to communicate but really doesn't.

Jeffrey Pfeffer and Robert Sutton, authors of *The Knowing-Doing Gap: How Smart Companies Turn Knowledge into Action,* refer to the "mystique of complexity," which encourages businesspeople to impress others with complex language and convoluted ideas. As a result, we scramble to create an aura of competence by using incomprehensible jargon. The practice, however, confuses people and inhibits action.

Particularly in large organizations, it's easy to mimic all those around you who are trying either to make the ordinary sound extraordinary or to shift responsibility. Once, when I was consulting with a large company to help one of its divisions develop some marketing case studies, I kept encountering a phrase that lacked a real-world definition. The only problem was that I couldn't find anyone in the company who could translate the concept into plain English. It turned out that a senior staff member had put the phrase into use and the troops had readily parroted it without a clue as to what it meant.

Don't be satisfied with accepting statements with murky meanings from others, and avoid sending such messages yourself. In your next meeting, ask participants who are liberally using jargon to define terms in plain language. Pfeffer and Sutton's anecdotal surveys reveal that when managers were asked to define such business buzzwords as "learning organization," "paradigm," and "business process reengineering," many of them were either unable to give any definition or struggled to supply an inadequate one.

Make only promises you intend to keep. Saying "no" or "I can't" can be difficult, but getting labeled as someone who can't be believed or relied on is worse. Just as passing a bad check makes it difficult to write another one at a store, making commitments that you can't or don't intend to keep creates a real deficit in relationships. Be careful the next time you say "I'll see what I can do," "I'll get back to you," or "I'll have this done by Friday." Once people get the message that you don't mean to do what you say, it will take a major effort to reconstruct your credibility.

Admit mistakes. "Credibility comes from a willingness to admit to faults and mistakes," observes a marketing communications manager with a large accounting firm. "People who are 'never wrong' aren't believable."

Admitting a mistake won't make you appear weak or increase your vulnerability; in fact, it renders you more approachable and sincere. Particularly if you are in a management or coaching situation, you can create a positive climate for growth by sharing some of your own mistakes and what you've learned with others who are currently struggling with an issue. Admitting that you made a flawed decision can earn you the respect of others and make them more willing to accept constructive criticism from you and to give you credit when you deserve it.

In a world of faux, being a person of credibility and substance is a critical asset. Most people seek relationships that can endure in an atmosphere of change and turbulence and naturally gravitate to those who earn and deserve their trust. Establishing and maintaining a reputation for honesty and consistency takes effort and vigilance, but the rewards are significant and long-term—both for you and those around you.

THE BOTTOM LINE

- ➤ Credibility comes from a combination of who we are and what we do—a healthy balance of character and competence.
- ➤ Credibility takes time to establish, and in some cases, only an instant to destroy.
- ➤ A significant step toward creating and maintaining your own credibility is mastering the art of straight talk.
- ➤ Keeping promises and admitting mistakes contribute to your credibility.

CHAPTER 3

Develop Your Gratitude Attitude

Say "Thank You" and Mean It

*S*ome time ago, I heard of a bride who refused to open her gifts at the shower her friends at work gave for her because she "didn't know what to say" when she opened each gift. Separately, a busy executive sent each staff member a twenty-five-pound turkey for Thanksgiving along with a personal note. He received thanks from about half of his employees.

In an age of perceived entitlement, saying "thank you" graciously seems to be on the back burner. We live in an era of increasingly demanding customers, coworkers, and clients. We believe that we deserve to get *what* we want, *when* we want it. And to a certain extent, that's fine—as long as this attitude doesn't diminish our sense of gratitude when we should express thanks to those who are generous to us or serve us in any way.

WHEN IN DOUBT

Saying thank you can take time and effort, and we've all probably had lapses in expressing gratitude. Sometimes we might even question whether a "thank you" is really necessary. Occasionally, it's hard to know just what response is appropriate. Here are a few gratitude dos and don'ts to consider when expressing thanks in public, professional, or personal situations.

Do

Concern yourself more with substance than form. The issue is not so much the form that the thank you takes as the spirit behind it.

Of course, certain guidelines apply. Some situations demand a formal note; other times, a telephone call or an e-mail is sufficient. And a face-to-face thank you, where you support your words with strong vocalics, pitch, pace, and positive affirming body language, can be the most powerful of all.

Today, e-mail and voice mail are acceptable vehicles for thanking people, particularly for business-related intangibles such as covering for you at a meeting or referring a new client to you. Just remember that e-mail, for all its efficiency and relative informality, is still written communication. Make sure that you take the same pains with your e-mail thank you as you would with a note written on fine stationery to make it thoughtful and sincere. Remember also that e-mail is never truly private. Keep the tone and content professional.

If you have received a gift or have been to someone's home for dinner, on the other hand, the handwritten note still wins and becomes even more special in our world of electronic communication. If you find yourself procrastinating because you find letter-writing a hassle, make it easier by keeping stationery, pens, and stamps in a single place where you can sit down and get it done all at once. Or, if finding the right words is difficult for you, stores and online card sites are full of appropriate thank-you cards to which you can add a personal comment and signature.

Respond quickly and enthusiastically. Whatever form you use, two attributes are critical, whether thanking someone for a kindness, a business lunch, or an expensive gift: timeliness and enthusiasm. The two actually create a powerful synergy: the quicker you respond, the more enthusiastic you will be. The one exception where you can cut yourself a little slack is with wedding gifts—most experts say it is acceptable to take up to three months to send a thank-you note. If you know that responding to all those gifts is going to take some time, devise a system for letting the giver know that you *did* receive it and that a more formal thank you will follow.

When timeliness becomes an impossible goal, remember that late is better than never. Don't think, "It's been so long I'd be embarrassed to thank him now." Apologize for the delay if you feel that's necessary, and then say thanks the same way you would have had no delay occurred.

In some situations, use the one-two punch. Because a quick response is usually more effective—and appreciated—busy people often find it convenient to make a telephone call immediately (even if you just leave a message) and then follow up with a note. The receiver benefits from the strengths of both channels of communication: the richness and spontaneity of the spoken message and the permanence and authority of the written form.

You can also follow up with an oral thank you *after* you've put it in writing. This verbal response doesn't have to be part of a formal process; you can simply do it when the occasion arises. For example, when you see the person next, you can reiterate your appreciation. A spontaneous comment makes people feel that your thanks are sincere and not just perfunctory adherence to protocol.

Learn to be a gracious receiver. You undoubtedly know that it's important to be a gracious giver, but what about being a gracious receiver? You've probably encountered people who, instead of simply expressing a sincere thank you, are compelled to repay a kindness in equal—or greater—measure.

Let's say, for example, that for your friends' anniversary you agreed to house-sit their lovely home, which came complete with a pool and fully stocked bar, while they had a much-needed long weekend getaway. You were happy to do it for them; that was your gift.

Upon their return, however, they thank you with a $200 gift certificate to the latest trendy restaurant, along with a huge bouquet of flowers. All of a sudden, you feel compelled to write a note of thanks for their thank you. Instead of being a willing giver, you are suddenly indebted to your friends for *their* generosity, and your act of kindness got lost in the shuffle.

For some people, allowing others to do something for them threatens their sense of self-sufficiency or exposes insecurity, so they respond in a way that they feel relieves them of any indebtedness. Don't fall into this trap. When someone does something kind or generous for you, the best way to show your gratitude is to sincerely tell the person how appreciative you are. Don't overshadow the kindness with your own magnanimity. We all need to learn to accept graciously; people feel affirmed when their gesture evokes a positive reaction. Making the giver feel good is in itself a gift. Of course, when the opportunity arises later, you can always repay the kindness.

Don't

Don't "damn with faint praise." Respond warmly and enthusiastically when someone does something special for you. Opening a gift box and remarking, "Oh, it's a tie," doesn't qualify as a wholehearted response. I'll always remember years ago when I sent a friend in another state a poinsettia for the holidays, wiring the purchase through a local florist. When I asked her if she had received the plant, she responded, "Oh yes, and I was really amazed at how nice it was. Usually when you wire flowers, the local florist sends the worst selection in the shop, since the buyer will never see it." Somehow, that response didn't have the same effect as "I loved the plant. It looks beautiful in my office."

Don't make the giver feel guilty. Some people, in saying thanks, actually end up making the giver feel as if he or she did something wrong or inappropriate. One I'll never forget is: "Thanks for the cake. Although I'm allergic to chocolate, I took my medicine and hoped for the best." Even something as "polite" as "Oh, you shouldn't have done this," or "I feel terrible that you went to so much trouble" can send a mixed message. It's fine, however, to acknowledge that someone went to considerable effort. Just keep the focus on the positive. For example, instead of saying, "Oh, you shouldn't have," say, "I know how hard you must have worked on this lovely afghan. It will always be special to me."

What if you really hate the gift, or just have no use for it? For example, if a colleague presents you with a gift for the holiday, let's say a scarf, but the scarf is just *not* your style and you can't imagine actually wearing it. Or you already have floral arrangements all perfectly arranged when someone shows up for your dinner party with a bouquet in hand? In such cases, try to concentrate on the motivation and focus the thanks around the thoughtfulness of the gesture rather than the item itself. Don't let the giver know that you are less-than-thrilled with the gift. Instead, focus on the act of giving and graciously thank the person for his or her thoughtfulness.

Even though we're told that giving is more beneficial than receiving, the act of receiving graciously is an attribute that we should all cultivate. People feel rewarded for their effort, and the positive reinforcement makes them more amenable to doing things for others. The result is a more civilized, more pleasant, and more considerate environment for all of us.

THE BOTTOM LINE

- ➤ Saying thank you often takes time and effort.
- ➤ It's easy to rationalize that we don't say thank you because we're too busy or we don't know what to say.
- ➤ The *form* of the thank you is less important than the *spirit* behind it.
- ➤ Timeliness and enthusiasm create a powerful synergy.
- ➤ Making the giver feel good is in itself a gift.
- ➤ Receiving graciously is an ability worth cultivating.

CHAPTER 4

Are Your Nonverbal Messages Telling on You?

You're in the middle of one of the most important presentations of your life. You have done extensive research to be sure you project confidence and authority. Your computer-generated slides are flawless. You're impeccably dressed. The information is simply rolling off your tongue. Things are going very well.

Then, as your eyes scan the room, they come to rest on the most important person in the audience—the decision-maker. His eyes are on the conference table. His fingers play aimlessly with a pen. He is swiveling back and forth in the chair. He stops playing with the pen long enough to pick some invisible lint off his sleeve.

You feel your mouth go dry and a cold sweat break out on your forehead. You try to get back into the swing of your presentation, but you can't take your eyes off Mr. Turned Off and Tuned Out. He might as well get up out of his chair and walk out of the room. His body language is saying it all.

When you engage in conversation or deliver a presentation, picking up on your audience's many and ongoing nonverbal signals will improve your chances of communicating successfully with them. Likewise, monitoring and tailoring your own body language will help you send a positive message and encourage your audience to be straightforward and responsive.

WHAT EXACTLY IS NONVERBAL COMMUNICATION?

Nonverbal communication includes so many areas that it may be easier to define what it *isn't* rather than what it is. According to Dr. Paul R.

Timm, in *Managerial Communication: A Finger on the Pulse*, most researchers agree that nonverbal communication includes everything except our use of words and numbers in written and oral communication. "The sobering reality," says Timm, "is that what we *say* is almost always overridden by what we *do*. Indeed, regardless of what words convey, our bodies tell others how we *feel* about what we say." As Carol Kinsey Goman explains in her book *The Silent Language of Leaders: How Body Language Can Help—or Hurt—How You Lead*, you might already know that leadership is about communication, "but did you also know that the people you're speaking to will have subliminally evaluated your credibility, confidence, likability, and trustworthiness in the first seven seconds—before you had a chance to deliver your well-rehearsed speaking points? Did you know that your use of personal space, physical gestures, posture, facial expressions, and eye contact could already have sabotaged your message?"

What we call nonverbal communication, or body language, includes stance, gestures, motion, facial expression (including eye contact), and use of personal space. Most experts agree that nonverbal communication also extends to makeup, clothing, jewelry, and personal possessions. Here are some examples of poor nonverbal communication:

➤ A manager looks at her computer screen when an employee is talking to her, obviously sending a message of disinterest or lack of time.

➤ An aggressive sales rep takes his seat at a conference table and spreads his papers on either side of him, intruding on the personal space of those seated beside him.

➤ A new employee wears flashy, expensive jewelry, perhaps hoping to impress her new colleagues.

We send strong messages, either positive or negative, through the things we do, which are often more powerful than words.

The Voice as Nonverbal Communication

The voice also makes up a critical component of a spoken message. It's not just *what* you say, but *how* you say it. The elements of pitch, pace, and power (volume, authority, passion) can project such qualities as timidity, hostility, confidence, suspicion, and collaboration. A monotone delivery may say to the audience that the speaker isn't really engaged in his or her topic.

"Fillers" such as "uh," "okay," and "you know," and hedging phrases such as "I think," "I feel," and "sort of," all undermine a speaker's authority and confidence.

Some speakers fall into the habit of "uptalk"—or ending a declarative statement with an upward inflection as though it were a question. People who use uptalk come across as powerless, and their speech sounds unsure. They appear to need constant validation and agreement from their audience.

THE POWER OF NONVERBAL COMMUNICATION

In the hierarchy of communication, spoken messages possess the most richness and flexibility because we can call on so many factors to deliver our ideas. When we are in someone's presence, we have both the verbal component and nonverbal assets that we can leverage for success. What may be surprising is that research shows that words are actually the smallest part of a message—dramatically overshadowed by the nonverbal components.

More specifically, words comprise a mere 7 percent to 10 percent of a spoken message. Nonverbal factors make up the remainder of the message, with the voice accounting for another 35 percent to 38 percent. The rest comes from body language.

What these findings mean is that when the verbal and nonverbal components of our messages are at odds with each other, it's no contest. The nonverbal factor will win every time. Too often, we send nonverbal messages without being aware of what we're telling those around us. So being oblivious to that part of our communication can truly sabotage the most carefully planned communication.

When Does Communication Begin?

We begin to send messages from the first moment we are in our listeners' presence. The way we enter a room, the way we make eye contact, the way we shake hands or nod in greeting, the way we take a seat and where we choose to sit, all send signals about whether we are friend or foe, knowledgeable or incompetent, confident or nervous.

Studies show that it takes less than a minute for us to react either positively or negatively to someone, and if that first impression is negative, several encounters are necessary to change that perception.

INTERPRETING NONVERBAL COMMUNICATION

Just as it's important for you to be aware of your own nonverbal communication and what it conveys to others, you must also be able to interpret others' nonverbal responses to your communication.

Be sensitive to the signals. In simple terms, we can categorize the "message" of body language by whether the audience seems to accept or reject our message and whether their response tends to be active or passive. The reaction can be described as illustrated in Figure 4-1.

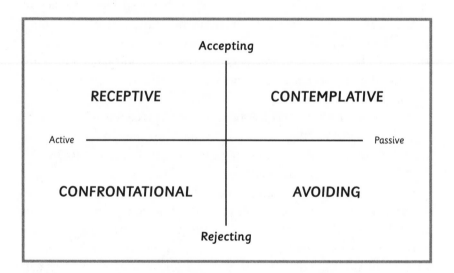

Figure 4-1. Adapted from John Mole, Mind Your Manners: Managing Business Cultures in the New Global Europe *3rd Edition.*

Someone who leans toward you and nods energetically with a pleasant facial expression, perhaps even a smile, sends a signal that he or she agrees with what you're saying and will probably approve your request or proposal. A tilted head and a body position that leans away from you, with more restrained body language, may be accepting but passive. This person is probably thinking about what you're saying and willing to hear more.

Like acceptance, rejection has its own nonverbal communication—either active or passive. In passive rejection, the body language becomes evasive and tries to create some distance. The eyes wander; the head turns away, the hands fidget. You get the distinct impression that the person has mentally left the room. You may not get a straight reaction from the words, but the message is coming through all the same. In such a situation, you may want to switch, at least temporarily, to a subject that you know is more pleasing to the person or ask questions to create some dialogue. Active rejection is a little easier to interpret. It may take the form of an intense sullen stare. Body language may look as though the person is gearing up for an attack. When you experience active rejection, find a way to determine why before continuing in your current direction, perhaps by speaking to the person in private.

If you're not sure, ask for clarification. As with any communication, the possibility for ambiguity in nonverbal communication often exists. For example, someone listening to you with his or her arms crossed, traditionally considered a negative signal, may simply be relaxed and comfortable with you. Avoid judging any one component in isolation. Look at the total package. If everything else looks positive, don't worry so much about a single nonverbal signal.

However, if you are getting a consistently negative message or see a sudden change in someone's demeanor, stance, or posture, it's often helpful to ask questions to find out why the person feels that way. If you're in a one-on-one situation, you might say, "Julie, you seem a bit uncomfortable with what I just said. Tell me what you're thinking." If you're in a group setting, then address the group and invite people with concerns to voice those concerns or to share their perspective.

COURTESY IS AS COURTESY DOES

Based on our understanding of the impact of nonverbal communication, it's not hard to accept that courtesy often begins with body language. And because the nonverbal component so outweighs the verbal component of our message, your actions will always speak louder than your words. Once when I was in a department meeting, a colleague suddenly closed her notebook and pushed her chair back, crossing her arms. No one at the table had trouble recognizing her displeasure at what the meeting leader had just said.

People sometimes use body language to intimidate, exclude, deni-grate, condescend, and humiliate. It's safer than actually communicat-ing those negative messages with words, because the meaning of the body language can be refuted and the message can simply be labeled a misinterpretation.

On the other hand, negative body language is often not deliberate and may just result from insensitivity. In a communication class that I was teaching, I led the students in a group decision-making exercise. Of eight students sitting around one rectangular table, all except one were male. In addition to being the only woman in the group, this stu-dent was also relatively new to the United States. She took a seat at the corner, which prevented her being able to draw her chair completely under the table.

As the discussion progressed, the two people sitting on either side of her shifted their bodies so that their backs were turned to her, in effect creating a circle from which she was excluded. At the same time, she leaned back in her chair and withdrew from the discussion.

In debriefing the group on some of their decision-making tech-niques, I showed them a video of their meeting. What caught every-one's attention was the group dynamics. The woman was offended by what she saw, and the other students were obviously embarrassed by their behavior. To a person, they all insisted that they had not acted deliberately. The results, however, were the same as if they had. It is equally true that the woman had not asserted herself during the con-versation. In fact, as the meeting progressed, she had become increas-ingly disengaged, thereby not contributing to the outcome.

Our nonverbal actions can also display concern, compassion, inter-est in, and respect for others. A smile and a nod as you pass someone in the hall, a hearty handshake to congratulate a colleague for a job well done, or obvious attentiveness to what someone is saying all fos-ter positive interpersonal relationships.

Even in an adversarial situation, the right nonverbal messages can defuse hostility. For example, maintaining a composed demeanor and restraining your own body language when someone is angry with you can actually have a calming effect on the person. Keeping your voice low, limiting gestures, and maintaining a relaxed posture will discour-age the other person from continuing to rant. On the other hand, dis-playing animation and enthusiasm with someone who is happy or excited can validate and support the person's feelings.

SYNCHRONIZE YOUR BODY LANGUAGE

Effective communication requires keeping your own body language in sync with that of the person with whom you're communicating. For example, if your body language naturally tends to be expressive and dramatic, your style is perfectly suitable for communicating with an animated, enthusiastic person. However, you probably should tone it down when in conversation with a particularly low-key or restrained person. The idea is to make sure that your body language doesn't make others uncomfortable because it either overpowers or underwhelms them. What if your own style tends to be restrained or low key? In that case, it's best to be yourself and not try to match the style of someone who tends to be more spirited. If you do try, you will probably feel uncomfortable and your communication will project a degree of insincerity.

COMMON BODY LANGUAGE AND ITS MEANING

To help you stay on track, here's a brief summary of some common body language signals and their meaning.

DEFENSIVE/CONFRONTATIONAL
- Arms crossed on chest
- Crossing legs
- Fist-like gestures
- Pointing index finger

REFLECTIVE
- Head tilted
- Stroking chin
- Peering over glasses
- Taking glasses off and cleaning

SUSPICIOUS
- Arms crossed
- Sideways glance
- Touching or rubbing nose
- Squinting slightly

OPEN AND COOPERATIVE
- Upper body in sprinter's position
- Open hands
- Sitting on edge of chair
- Tilted head
- Hands behind back
- Steepled hands

INSECURE AND NERVOUS
- Chewing pen or pencil
- Biting fingernails
- Hands in pockets
- Clearing throat repeatedly
- Pinching or picking skin or clothing
- Fidgeting in chair
- Hand covering mouth while speaking
- Poor eye contact
- Perspiring
- Tugging at ear
- Playing with hair
- Swaying

FRUSTRATED
- Short breaths
- Tightly clenched hands
- Pointing index finger
- Rubbing hand through hair
- Rubbing back of neck

Knowing the Principles Eliminates Mixed Messages

As you strive to communicate more clearly, understanding nonverbal communication can be a tremendous asset in your professional as well as personal communications. Being deliberate in your nonverbal communication and clearly interpreting and appropriately responding to the nonverbal cues of others will ensure that others *see* as well as *hear* what you're saying.

THE BOTTOM LINE

- ➤ Recognizing and understanding other people's nonverbal signals is critical to communicating successfully with them.
- ➤ Monitoring and tailoring your own body language will help you send a positive message and encourage your audience to be straightforward and responsive.
- ➤ What you *say* is almost always overridden by what you *do*. Body language tells others how you *feel* about what you say.
- ➤ Your voice makes up a critical component of a spoken message.
- ➤ Courtesy often begins with body language.
- ➤ Nonverbal awareness can minimize or eliminate mixed messages and misunderstandings.

CHAPTER 5

What the $%#*!& Is Going on Here?

*F*rom the beach to the boardroom, and everywhere in between, our sound waves sizzle with curse words, sexual references, and crude colloquialisms. In business, social, and institutional settings, it sometimes seems that anything goes when it comes to what we say. In her research at Georgia State University's Robinson College of Business, Dr. Carol White found that even the hallowed halls of academia ring with an unmistakable increase in cursing, references to the human anatomy, and offensive slang, among both students and faculty. Among students who responded to her survey, 47 percent saw nothing wrong with cursing in class. When you consider the proliferation of profanity in movies, music, and other entertainment media, it's easy to recognize the shift in social norms regarding language.

OBSCENITY GOES MAINSTREAM

At one time, people reserved swearing for those times that they hit their finger with the hammer, wrecked their car, or discovered a negative balance in their checking account. Today, we curse colorfully when we are surprised, delighted, amused, frightened, puzzled, concerned, or sympathetic. It's become an integral part of the speech patterns of many people of all ages and upbringing.

Without a doubt, language once considered vulgar or taboo has become socially acceptable—probably for a variety of reasons. Even in professional settings, people have become more comfortable with explicit language. Perhaps the shift came about because we spend so much time with strangers. At one time, a vast number of people lived most of their lives in a close-knit community where everyone knew everyone else. In such a setting, there was strong motivation to always be on one's best behavior. When surrounded by people with whom they have a personal, even if casual, relationship, people are more concerned about the impression they make and how they are perceived. Today, however, it's more likely that when you are out in public, you are anonymous, barely noticed by other people busily going about their lives. In such an environment, there's less motivation to make a good impression or to care about being offensive. A human resources manager with a major telecommunications firm once commented to me, "Quite often, when I travel, I'm amazed at what I hear coming from the person on a cell phone standing right next to me. It's as if that person thinks no one else is around."

Other factors contributing to the increase in public profanity include the entertainment media. Censorship barriers have gradually fallen so that what used to be unthinkable language or content in movies on television, on radio, or in other mass media has become so commonplace that most of us hardly notice it. As we've become desensitized to vulgar language, it's no wonder so many of us don't see the harm in cursing and swearing.

THE PROFESSIONAL COST OF CURSING

Because cursing is often tolerated by society, many of us may believe that crude speech is really no big deal. Admittedly, some articles even cite studies that assert that profanity can create a communal atmosphere at work that encourages teamwork and solidarity.

However, if you believe that we now have complete freedom to use profanity in your professional communication, eventually you will face negative consequences.

IS VULGARITY A FIRST AMENDMENT RIGHT?

Many people consider the right to swear anywhere and everywhere part of the freedom-of-speech package. Although you may believe that the First Amendment gives you the right to use whatever words suit you, you should also be aware of the impact your words have on others and of what they communicate about you. Here are a few points to keep in mind.

Don't take it for granted that you won't offend others. Because our speech patterns become habitual, we often use words and phrases without giving much thought to how they sound to others. Therefore, be aware that what may seem perfectly harmless to you may be shocking to someone else.

Consider your audience. If you're watching a ball game with a bunch of college buddies, being excited and enthusiastic probably won't raise any eyebrows. On the other hand, if you're in a meeting with clients, chances are that swearing will offend at least some—if not all—of your audience. If you curse in a setting where you are expected to be professional and polished, it's likely that your audience will decide you are incompetent and boorish. Needless to say, such an image will not enhance your professional success.

Watch your language in public places. When you're in a packed stadium at a sporting event, on a subway, in a crowded elevator, or in a theater, you are sharing space with people of varying demographics, values, and standards. Just as you would practice general conventions of courtesy in these situations, such as not pushing, cutting in line, or belching loudly, you should also consider how your words might be an offense to others. As a rule, when in public, keep your voice down, use your phone with discretion, avoid explicit or intimate conversations, and choose a neutral vocabulary that minimizes the possibility of offending, angering, or embarrassing those within earshot.

Never use offensive speech as a show of power or to intimidate. A manager in a major media company remarked to me that certain senior officers of her firm were fond of conducting profanity-peppered conversations on crowded elevators. They seemed to think that since they are the power players in the corporation, other people have to put up with their crudeness, like it or not.

Those who curse or use offensive language around subordinates and coworkers may be indulging in a form of verbal bullying that borders on abuse. Aside from creating an unpleasant environment, this behavior also carries legal risks, as it can easily be construed as harassment.

Remember good judgment is always in good taste. Although there are situations when profanity might be tolerated or excused, the only safe choice is to forgo a curse and express your feelings—whether you're angry or elated or anywhere in between—in another way. When it comes to your professional success, developing this habit may affect you in ways that you're not even aware of. Although most people may not react overtly to your use of obscenities, your words may at some point offend someone who can make or break your career. On the other hand, if your language is always courteous and polished, this might be the trait that gives you the edge when promotion decisions are being made.

THE BOTTOM LINE

- ➤ For many reasons, offensive language has become ubiquitous in public life.
- ➤ In spite of a social desensitization toward vulgarity and a growing tolerance of it, using obscene words and phrases can still have a negative social and professional impact.
- ➤ Even if you believe the First Amendment protects your right to use obscenities, you should also be aware of the impact your words have on others and on your image.
- ➤ Be sensitive to the needs and rights of others.
- ➤ The person you offend may be someone who can affect your career.
- ➤ Courteous and polished language is always a safe choice.

CHAPTER 6

Tell Me Less

Some Things Are Better Left Unsaid

An e-mail goes to everyone in the company, announcing the birth of a baby—and giving more than a few details about the wife's protracted labor.

The woman who works on your floor corners you at an office party and tells you more about her dysfunctional relationship with her mother than people usually tell their analysts.

A loquacious manager turns small talk before a meeting into a play-by-play description of the ugly details of his recent divorce.

*P*erhaps the blurring of the boundaries when it comes to keeping some things private is attributable to the age in which we live, when exhaustive information on just about any topic is just a few keystrokes away. Social media enables us to reveal details about our lives through words, photos, and even videos. We have a constant audience, and at times people become competitive regarding how much and how quickly they can tell us about their most mundane activities.

Perhaps it's because so many barriers have come down—physical barriers in offices, geographical barriers, and emotional barriers as we grow accustomed to the tell-all mentality of the modern media. Or possibly it's because we've never been so connected—and yet so disconnected. At work, this environment often means that you find out more about your coworkers than you really want to know. Whether it's your neighbor in the next cubicle stopping in for a chat and telling you about her ongoing dispute with her sister-in-law, or a coworker sharing too freely the details of his recent string of dates, it seems that some people don't know how to censor their own communications.

REBUILDING THE BOUNDARIES AT WORK

Offices without walls and flatter organizations can make maintaining social and professional barriers at work a challenge. Furthermore, cell phones, texting, instant messaging, and e-mail also create a kind of "in your face" communication approach that chips away at the distance between us—a distance that sometimes can be healthy. This lack of privacy encourages an artificial intimacy that we may grow to regret and resent.

All around us we see the effects of living in an age of no-holds-barred self-disclosure. From TV talk or "reality" shows to shock jocks on the radio, no subject today seems to be off-limits in casual conversation. Some people seem intent on exposing the most intimate sides of their own and other people's lives to anyone who will listen. Yet even when we're bombarded with answers to questions we haven't asked and receive more information from people than we want, we're reluctant to complain for fear of offending the speaker. Although open and honest communication certainly is a valuable component in any relationship—business or personal—there is such a thing as being too open and honest.

BALANCING OPENNESS AND PRIVACY

Self-revelation helps us define ourselves to others. It provides insights into our personal feelings and emotions and helps other people get to know us and relate to us. For example, when you tell a coworker that you just moved to the area from another part of the country, or that you are new to your current profession and that you used to be a teacher, you are letting the other person see you as more than just "the new sales rep" or "the marketing manager," adding another dimension to your identity.

Self-disclosure traditionally leads to increased familiarity and, in the right environment, increases over time. However, people sometimes forgo the natural progression of a relationship and try to attain instant intimacy, perhaps mistaking that for friendship. For some people this may stem from a need to fill an emotional void or from a misguided belief that their openness will endear them to others. For other people, "oversharing" may simply be a result of a poor understanding of what is socially acceptable. In our warp-speed world, when we're often in a job or a city for a short time or we're dealing with people via cyberspace, we push for instant intimacy—and sometimes we move too quickly for someone's comfort level.

Although revealing information about yourself may help you build bridges with coworkers, you must maintain a balance between being open and maintaining an appropriate level of privacy. Furthermore, you need to recognize just how much information other people are really interested in hearing. Self-disclosure has its place and in many cases can build bridges between people and strengthen relationships. We need, however, to take a thoughtful approach that considers everyone involved. Here are some general rules to keep in mind.

Think before you share or write. Revealing sensitive information about yourself may seem like a good idea in the moment, but in the cold light of day you may regret it. I've had people tell me intimate secrets only to end up feeling awkward and uncomfortable around me afterward.

Revealing personal information can become especially risky when you put it in writing, because once it reaches its destination, the message is out of your control. You are especially vulnerable when you send e-mail since the receiver could choose to forward your message to others. Before you hit the "Send" button, stop and consider for a moment if you're completely comfortable with the information in the e-mail, no matter who ends up reading it.

Avoid gossip. Sharing too much information sometimes involves sharing personal information about others. If you are privy to a secret about one of your coworkers, whether it's of a professional or personal nature, keep that information to yourself. Let's face it: No one likes a gossip. Even when your audience is receptive to what you're revealing, it's likely that your trustworthiness will become suspect, and you will be seen as a gossipy busybody. Likewise, when someone comes to you with personal information about a colleague, politely but firmly let the person know that you don't feel that this information concerns you and that you'd rather not hear it. Respect other people's privacy, and don't share information about them that they wouldn't share themselves.

Stay away from topics that may be off-limits. Keep in mind that certain subjects, such as religious beliefs, personal finances, details about illnesses and mental health, or personal details about a marriage, divorce, or affair, may make other people uncomfortable. If someone you only know casually asks about your health, for example, keep your answer short and general, avoiding a detailed account of a specific medical problem.

Watch the listener's reaction. Some people are more open than others to receiving unexpected personal information. Watch your listener's nonverbal response as you speak. An uncomfortable listener may not say anything, but the person's body language should make matters abundantly clear. Watch for a change in stance, eye contact, or facial expression; sudden fidgeting such as playing with hands or a nearby object; and noncommittal or vague responses. In such cases, recognize that your listener may not want to hear what you have to say. Drop the subject once and for all and move on to a new topic.

TEN TOPICS TO AVOID IN WORKPLACE CONVERSATIONS

Detailed health problems
Details of sex life
Problems with spouse/partner
Personal finances (either positive or negative)
Personal religious views
Hot political topics that evoke passion
Personal lives of other coworkers
Gossip about the boss
Jokes that disparage other ethnic, racial, or religious groups
Lavish purchases

Don't expect or demand reciprocity. Studies have shown that when we reveal personal information about ourselves, we often expect the other party to give us some juicy information in return. And if we are honest with ourselves, we have to admit that we are disappointed when our audience doesn't reciprocate. In the workplace, sharing confidences may seem to be a way to strengthen a professional relationship when in reality we may simply want to satisfy our own curiosity about another person.

If you are inclined to bare your soul, recognize your audience's right not to do so in return. Similarly, when you happen to be on the receiving end of the conversation, don't let yourself get trapped into feeling obligated to provide equally personal information about yourself.

In some cases, get the other person's okay before proceeding. Preface your remarks with a statement that allows your audience to choose whether or not to hear what you have to say. You might say to the other person, "What I'm about to tell you is highly personal. Let me know if you'd rather we not go there." If the listener shows the slightest hesitation, even if he or she doesn't tell you directly, change the subject willingly and move quickly to a less sensitive topic. Be sure to divert the conversation graciously, moving on to a neutral topic without making the other person feel guilty for not listening to you.

WHEN YOU ARE THE RECIPIENT OF UNWANTED INFORMATION

When you're feeling that you are getting too much information, let the other person know it up-front. For example, if a coworker with whom you have only a professional relationship begins to discuss his dating habits with you and this information not only doesn't interest you but also makes you feel uncomfortable, politely bring the subject to a close. Although you may feel uncomfortable speaking up, doing so is better than letting things go too far. However, be sure to keep your reaction light and nonjudgmental so that the speaker doesn't feel embarrassed about what he or she has already disclosed. You might use humor as a way to let the person tactfully know you'd rather not hear anymore. Another approach might be to simply change the subject.

WHAT YOU *DON'T* SAY TELLS A LOT

In the end, being sensitive to others and choosing when and where to divulge personal information is itself a form of self-revelation. Knowing just how much to share—about yourself and others—might just be one of the biggest indicators of your character. It might mean the difference between your being viewed by coworkers as tactless, insensitive, or just plain clueless, and being seen as a professional who respects other people's privacy and recognizes the importance of maintaining appropriate personal space at work.

THE BOTTOM LINE

- ➤ In an age in which exhaustive information on just about any topic is just a few keystrokes away, we can easily forget how much information is too much.
- ➤ Flatter organizations, offices without walls, and technology can make it a challenge to maintain barriers at work.
- ➤ Self-disclosure has its place and can strengthen relationships, but it's important to balance openness with privacy.
- ➤ Use good judgment about how much to share with others and how much to tolerate hearing when you're on the receiving end.
- ➤ Remember that you can't unsay what you reveal.
- ➤ What you *don't* say can tell a lot about you.

CHAPTER 7

Giving *Genuine* Compliments That Count

*T*he philosopher William James once said, "The deepest principle in human nature is the craving to be appreciated." Xenophon, the ancient Greek philosopher and historian, tells us, "The sweetest of all sounds is praise."

THE POWER OF PRAISE

The fact that people respond positively to accolades is not a revelation. Even though we may not readily admit it, most of us enjoy recognition for our good deeds, accomplishments, and hard work. The positive reinforcement inspires us to keep meeting the challenges and difficulties we face daily.

Yet when given without sincerity, praise might be taken for flattery or manipulation, and the person giving that kind of praise will quickly earn a reputation for being a brownnoser or a bootlicker. Always telling your boss what a wonderful job he did eventually comes across as insincere and is irritating.

When sincere, praise can be a powerful tool for motivating others. People feel valued and recognized for what they are doing well, and often a genuine compliment inspires a person to strive for additional achievement.

GIVING PRAISE

How can you avoid the traps that cheapen the praise you offer and instead give praise in a way that increases others' sense of self-worth and motivates them to new levels of purpose and accomplishment?

Here are a few tips to make sure that your positive feedback is genuine and that you engage and inspire others in the process.

Praise, don't flatter. American poet Phyllis McGinley calls praise an "earned thing." It usually results from something we have done to deserve the commendation. Feedback, given honestly, is the kind of praise that reinforces and rewards success because it focuses on a specific action. For example: "The invitation you designed for the fundraiser is really getting a lot of attention and positive comments. Thanks for sharing your artistic talents." Generally speaking, flattery is excessive or unwarranted praise, with little substance: "You're always so professional! You're a real inspiration," is a good illustration of words that flatter.

Staying focused on the action rather than the person is a good way to avoid having our praise perceived as empty flattery. Furthermore, people feel more comfortable accepting compliments about what they have done rather than about who they are. There are exceptions, of course. For example, you may want to pay tribute to someone's cool head in a crisis or some other behavioral attribute. Yet even in those situations it's best to tie the remarks to a particular performance to increase their validity. If others are present when you are giving a compliment, you won't run the risk of appearing to play favorites if you are remarking about a verifiable event.

Be specific. Often, people limit praise to vague, general statements, but give pointed, specific criticism. We've all known the boss who walks around saying "good job" to everyone in a one-size-fits-all response. Obviously, all contributions aren't equal, but in this approach, both the outstanding accomplishment and the marginal performance receive similar accolades. No one feels singled out, and the manager's credibility suffers. Perhaps worse, those who really do outstanding work and make an extra effort don't feel that their managers recognize singular contributions. For your praise to count, be sure that your positive feedback is just as specific as any negative comment you give.

Focus on the receiver. Praise people in a style that's consistent with the recipient's personality. You can't understand why Janet didn't react well to the award you presented her in the department meeting this morning. She seemed particularly uncomfortable when everyone shouted, "Speech! Speech!" In fact, you're a bit miffed about her lack of enthusiasm. She hardly thanked you.

The maxim of "praise in public and reprimand in private" doesn't necessarily hold true in every situation. Some people would also like to receive praise in private because they are easily embarrassed by the public attention, or they may worry about the resentment that the recognition might spark. On the other hand, many people love the spotlight. They would be happy if you hired a marching band and turned on the klieg lights. Most people, obviously, fall somewhere in between. Make sure that you offer praise in a way that is in sync with individual personalities.

Don't undercut your words. Avoid following a compliment with a verbal jab, even if you mean it in fun. For example, "You did a great job smoothing Mr. Carter's ruffled feathers and saving the account. Not bad for an engineer." Or, "Your office is so clean, I thought I was in the wrong place!" Even people who appreciate a good joke or enjoy a convivial ribbing still prefer an unsullied compliment. Let the person enjoy the moment without associating it with something even slightly negative.

Make sure that you don't use the encounter as a "teaching moment." Too often we let negative feedback creep into a conversation about what someone has done well. "Manuel, that was a great presentation. If you had shortened it by ten minutes, it would have been even better."

Avoid excessive praise of the boss. Use good judgment in praising higher-ranking colleagues. Everyone—at every level in the corporate hierarchy—needs kind words. However, in giving praise, especially to someone in power, you must be sincere and your compliment needs to be free of a hidden agenda. Perhaps your manager had to make a particularly difficult announcement to the department about impending layoffs and she handled the difficult topic clearly and compassionately. Although complimenting her for handling day-to-day activities is generally inappropriate, she is likely to appreciate your positive response to her difficult task. Heaping praise on a superior can create suspicion—in both the person on the receiving end and anyone else within earshot—so your words must come across as genuine.

When praising someone higher up in the organization, keep the focus on a specific behavior or benefit, and pick your spots carefully to deliver these compliments. If you're there with a gushy commendation every time the boss speaks to the troops, you will develop a reputation for being a sycophantic and self-serving.

Don't praise as a prelude to a request. Author and consultant Dianna Booher warns that too often, praise is a prelude for some kind of appeal. "Tom, your presentation on the new product was a show-stopper! Can you have a great sales pitch ready for our client in Denver day after tomorrow?" In this case, the kind words lose their effectiveness when they are used as a way to warm the person to a request. When you give praise, let the praise stand alone so that the recipient can savor the moment. If you need to ask the person for an additional favor or action, wait until later. Make the request a separate event.

PRAISE AS FEEDBACK

Praise is an important stimulus to our development. Managers, coworkers, parents, and partners frequently operate on the premise that silence means approval. That is, if everything's fine, you won't hear anything. More often, however, people find a lack of response to their actions deflating. It's a little bit like trying to carry on a conversation and not getting an answer from the person to whom you're speaking. Feedback is important. People need to know that they are on track and making progress just as much as they need to know when they go astray.

ACCEPTING PRAISE

Just as delivering praise effectively can spread goodwill and inspire positive behavior, accepting praise graciously is also a skill worth perfecting. Don't respond to a compliment by putting yourself down with a self-deprecating statement. While modesty can be a virtue, don't overdo it. Avoid responding to a compliment by saying, "Oh, it was no big deal." Instead, keep your reaction simple and direct with a reply such as, "Thank you. I'm glad the situation turned out well." By automatically returning a compliment, you are diluting the praise you received. So show restraint and offer your accolade later, when it will sound sincere rather than obligatory.

THE BOTTOM LINE

➤ One of the deepest principles in human nature is the craving to be appreciated.

➤ Praise might be mistaken for flattery or manipulation if it is not delivered with sincerity.

➤ Sincere praise can be a powerful tool for motivating others.

➤ Focus praise on a specific action, not on the person.

➤ Praise should be delivered in a way suited to the receiver's personality.

➤ Be judicious in praising those higher up in the workplace hierarchy.

➤ Accepting praise graciously is as important as giving it appropriately.

CHAPTER 8

Improving Your Listening Skills

"I missed that announcement. When did that happen?"
"Are you sure you told me about the change in location?"
"I didn't hear a thing about the new policy."
"You never listen to me. I might as well be talking to a wall socket."

*I*n a world of almost unlimited communication modes and wireless devices all around us, making them all but ubiquitous, we seem to be sorely lacking one of our most critical communication skills: listening. We have to admit that our culture does not encourage listening. Talk show guests and interviewers fight each other to be heard, speaking all at once. We talk on the telephone while surfing the Web, sending e-mails, or watching TV. Workplace "conversations" take place amid all kinds of competition for our attention—the computer screen, that stack of mail on our desk, the intriguing argument going on in the next cubicle.

Although we give lip service to its importance, listening gets little attention in a society that rewards the talker. Someone once said that conversation has become a competitive sport where the first person to draw a breath is declared the listener and thus relegated to the sideline. Indeed, we often view listening as a nonactivity. We state our intention not to participate in the meeting by saying that we're just going to "listen."

In the now-classic Rankin Study at Ohio State University, Paul Rankin discovered that listening makes up about 45 percent of our total communication activity, and yet we have almost no formal training in the act of paying rapt attention when someone else has the floor. We learn in school how to read, how to write, how to make speeches, and how to debate. How many of us ever took an academic course in developing the ability to listen to each other?

LISTENING FOR SUCCESS

The costs of not listening can run high. In addition to missing important information, you may fail to recognize problems or impending crises, and you may turn off friends, coworkers, clients, and family members. People quickly recognize that what they have to say doesn't count much with someone who is interested only in talking People who talk excessively without taking time to listen come across as self-absorbed and egotistical—and perhaps indeed they are.

The following recommendations may help you become a more effective listener.

Learn to want to listen. Contrary to conventional wisdom, listening is anything but passive. It requires an enormous amount of mental energy, concentration, desire, and a certain degree of unselfishness. We must commit to using our intellectual and emotional vitality to focus on hearing what someone has to say and then to process that information accurately and completely. Given that we think at a speed of about 500 words per minute and most people speak at a rate of about 150 words per minute, one might suppose that we would use that excess time to digest and integrate the data. On the contrary, our minds usually grab the available seconds to think about something else.

Deciding that listening is an important skill that you need and want to develop is the first step toward being a better listener.

Listen with more than your ears. You would be wise to listen with your eyes, mind, and heart, in addition to your ears, because the message consists of more than the words. Are the speaker's facial expressions, eye contact, and posture consistent with his or her words, or are you receiving mixed signals? Do the words say "I'm on board" while the body language says "I'd rather be anywhere but here"?

The verbal portion of a message is often just the tip of the iceberg. If you tend to accept everything at its most literal and surface level, you may miss the more important meanings behind the words. "We ran into a little glitch" might actually mean, "The chances of our being ready for this big demo are slim to none."

In any listening situation, be sure to listen for the facts and to read the nonverbal signals.

Identify and eliminate distractions. Distractions stem from both internal and external sources. Perhaps a family matter is concerning you, or you are super excited about your upcoming trip to Costa Rica. Maybe you woke up with a migraine, or the blaster burrito you had for lunch is playing havoc with your digestive system. Or you've got the presentation of your life in an hour and you can't stop obsessing over it.

Let's face it. Sometimes, no matter how commendable our intentions, we just aren't in the frame of mind to concentrate on what someone is saying. If you find yourself in this situation, consider making an appointment to listen at a later time. "Joe, I'm sorry, but I'm still fuming about what a jerk that customer can be. Give me a half-hour to decompress and debrief the boss, and then I'll be able to give you my full attention."

Most people would appreciate your honesty and be flattered that you care enough about what they have to say to find a better time to listen.

Be aware of and control your hot buttons. No matter how open-minded we claim to be, we all carry emotional baggage that interferes with our ability to listen. William Isaacs, consultant and author of *Dialogue: The Art of Thinking Together*, calls it "listening from disturbance," meaning we listen from our emotional memories rather than the current moment. Words, phrases, and voice inflections—even a person's appearance—can trigger negative reactions that shut down our receptivity. For example, the woman making a presentation who looks and sounds alarmingly like your Aunt Carmella, whose visits you always dreaded, is going to face a particular challenge getting through to you. And since she has no clue about your private hang-ups, she can't take action to neutralize them.

Recognize your personal listening inhibitors and develop a game plan to minimize their effects. Develop your ability to separate a legitimate reaction from a knee-jerk reflex, and focus on overcoming the latter when you're listening. For example, if a certain tone of voice or trite expression always sets you off, commit to getting past it and listening to what the speaker has to say.

Avoid appearing superior or condescending. Being a good listener puts you in the unique position of affirming another person in an active way, but it also opens up countless possibilities for your own development. Don't presume that what another person is saying will be irrelevant or that the person can't possibly tell you anything you don't already know. What you have to say comes from the information, knowledge, and wisdom that you have already accumulated. When you listen, however, you expand your horizons, increase your understanding, and might even gather material for the time when you are doing the talking.

Above all, listening shows respect for another person, and being a good listener enables you to forge strong relationships that can deliver long-term benefits.

THE BOTTOM LINE

- ➤ Listening gets little attention in a society that rewards the talker.
- ➤ Listening is anything but passive; it requires mental energy, concentration, commitment, and a certain degree of unselfishness.
- ➤ To be a better listener, eliminate distractions and control your emotional hot buttons.
- ➤ Realize that learning comes from listening.

CHAPTER 9

Being Smart About Smartphones and Other Devices

*Y*ou can find a restaurant and make a reservation in a click. You can make an appointment, share a photo, post to your social media site, and set the temperature in your house from a thousand miles away. The airline can send your boarding pass right to your phone. You can deposit your paycheck while sitting in the stands at a sporting event. Your e-mails are always at your fingertips, and every phone number you have in your contacts list is a touch away.

Furthermore, texting has become a mode of communication in itself, particularly among younger smartphone users. A 2011 study by Pew Research found that "fully 95 percent of 18- to 29-year-olds use the text messaging feature on their phones, and these users send or receive an average of 87.7 text messages on a normal day."

In a relatively few years, we have embraced smartphones and tablets to the point that we can't imagine life without them. From the mundane to the life-changing, we grab our smartphones for almost any situation. It's great to be able to let someone know that you're stuck in traffic and will be late for a meeting. And these devices can be lifesavers when we are in unfamiliar surroundings, having car trouble, or confronting an emergency. With a smartphone in hand, we're in touch and in control.

Smartphones have made us more efficient in countless ways, but they have also taken over our lives in many cases. The trick is to stay in command of this amazing tool without letting it become either a crutch or an impediment to our effective interaction with others.

Some time ago, I was invited to a "meet and greet" luncheon designed to bring together two organizations that saw opportunities for mutual benefit. When I arrived at the location and the elevator door opened, I saw four people standing in different parts of the small lobby. Instead of "meeting and greeting," all of them had their attention focused on whatever was happening on the screen of their individual phones, thereby missing the opportunity to begin the networking process.

And it's not just a U.S. obsession. While attending a conference in Europe a few years ago, I noticed that surprisingly few attendees seemed to be conversing with other people at the conference. At every break in the proceedings, scores of people whipped cell phones out of their pockets and handbags and, ignoring everyone around them, talked to someone elsewhere. Today, everywhere you look, people are engaged in cell phone conversations on the street and in cars, offices, shops, restaurants, airports, buses, and trains.

Cell phone use has become so ubiquitous that we seem to have forgotten that some phone behaviors in public aren't always okay. People place and take calls or send texts in the theater during a performance, in meetings and classes, in the hospital, during religious services, and in the middle of conversations we're trying to have with them. Have these handy devices become an actual necessity or are they just one more way for us to be rude to each other?

Perhaps we rely on these devices to overcome our discomfort in awkward or unfamiliar situations. Notice the next time that you get on an elevator. How many people in the car immediately grab their phones to check e-mails, even though they probably checked them a couple of minutes ago. Do they really feel that they can't take a forty-second ride to their office or their appointment without confirming that they received an e-mail in the last thirty seconds?

According to Mashable Statista, the average adult American spends one hour and nine minutes on a smartphone each day.

NEW RULES FOR A NEW GAME

So, what standards can we apply to make sure that we are using these tools in a way that enhance our professional image rather than making us look inept and immature?

Avoid allowing your devices to interfere with opportunities to interact with others. When you're there, *be there.* In most cases, unless someone is having a baby or you are waiting to hear from your important interview, face-to-face trumps electronic communication. If you are in a meeting or at a business lunch, put your phone on totally silent (no vibrating) and tuck it away in your pocket or handbag. If you place or take a phone call when you're engaged in a face-to-face meeting or conversation, you send a clear message to the person with you that someone on the cell is more important. Few issues can't wait an hour or two for resolution, and you always have voice mail and "missed call" notifications.

If, however, you are expecting a game-changing call, let the people around you understand that you may have to take it during your time together, and apologize for being unable to avoid the intrusion. Otherwise, focus solely on the people around you.

Even in less organized situations, be savvy about how you may be missing an opportunity to make important connections if you concentrate on your device rather than what's going on around you. Always be on the lookout for opportunities to make a good impression with those who are in your presence. Furthermore, you need to be alert to your surroundings at all times, particularly when you are in a situation where too much distraction may make you vulnerable to danger.

Think about what annoys you about other people's cell phone habits. Then make sure you don't commit equally aggravating offenses. Does the loud talker (or laugher) give you a headache? Do you feel trapped into listening to someone's sales call report in the elevator or the airport shuttle? Do you wish people wouldn't call from the stall in public restrooms? Does a coworker's ringtone drive you to distraction? Is the person ranting on the sidewalk using Bluetooth or is he just deranged?

Notice the habits that irritate you and consider your own behaviors. Particularly, if at all possible, carry on private conversations in a private place. Most people have their own issues to deal with; they don't need to be subjected to a stranger's haggling with a spouse over having to work late, admonishing kids to do their homework, or trying to arrange a date for the weekend. When talking on the phone, we often get so caught up in the phone call that we tune out to the fact that others around us are hearing everything we say (and even have a fairly good idea of what's happening on the other end of the line). If you're going to be discussing a personal matter, wait until you are alone.

Consider the needs of the other person. Make an effort to know the habits and preferences of those with whom you interact. Even if you favor texting, when you know that someone favors a live conversation, make a phone call. When a caller leaves you a voice mail, listen to it before you just return the missed call. Too often, I'm guilty of responding to the "missed call" message and ignoring the voice mail. Sometimes the person, obviously irritated, will ask, "Didn't you listen to my message?"

Speaking of voice mail, you may think that having your five-year-old record your greeting is adorable, but most callers would prefer a professional greeting that comes from you and gives concise information about how to proceed. Catchy or suggestive instructions related to leaving a message may be fine for your intimate associates ("You know what to do. Do it!), but remember that everyone, including your boss or a potential client, may choose to leave you a voice mail and may prefer something more businesslike.

Because smartphones are with us wherever we go, ask the person if it's a good time to talk and reschedule the call if necessary. Be respectful of time zone differences when you have that information. Many of us have received calls at 4:00 a.m. because the caller's time zone is during regular business hours. Obviously, you can't always know where someone may be, so the traveler needs to turn off his or her phone to avoid an unexpected wake-up call.

Avoid inconveniencing others because you are on the phone. Disconnect when you are in the checkout line at the grocery store, going through the quick service drive-through, or picking up your best friend's birthday cake, for example. When you can't carry on ordinary business operations efficiently because you won't stop your conversation, you inconvenience everyone around you—and increase your chances of getting the wrong amount of change or walking away without your credit card.

Unfortunately, the lack of consideration has become so pervasive that businesses have resorted to posting signs asking people not to use their cells when transacting business.

Observe guidelines for texting. The general guidelines for voice calls apply to text messages. Everyone knows that we shouldn't text while driving, and a number of states have made it illegal. Texting behind the wheel is even more dangerous than carrying on a distracting phone call. Dana Holmes, a lifestyle, gift, and etiquette expert, adds that we should not text anyone *we know* is driving.

Some additional principles of etiquette about texting are beginning to emerge.

If you are texting in a business environment, pay attention to spelling and grammar, just as you should in an e-mail. Avoid text lingo when sending a message to your chief operations officer: "Hi, Al. Great 2 meet u. BTW, r u hiring?"

The Emily Post Institute warns not to send anything of a confidential or intimate nature via text. We have seen glaring examples of how that practice can go terribly wrong. Remember that a text is still written communication and, like e-mail, it can go to the wrong person or persons quite easily.

Also, when texting someone who doesn't know you or have your phone number handy, write your name (Hi, I'm Jennifer from Dr. Stokes' office) at the beginning of the text.

Check your text before you hit send. The auto-correct feature can be either hilarious or embarrassing.

Avoid trashing anyone via text. I spoke with an executive who sent a text complaining about her staff's incompetence on a project. She sent it to a "trusted" colleague who passed the information along to the recipients of the criticism, doing serious damage to the manager's relationship with her team. Avoid sending texts, like e-mails, when you are angry or otherwise emotional. You can't always repair the damage.

Smartphones enhance our lives in ways we never dreamed possible. Remember, however, that they are tools and therefore are only as effective as the people who use them.

THE BOTTOM LINE

> ➤ Smartphones have changed our lives significantly for the better.
> ➤ Using a device as an exclusive communication tool can create superficial communication and hamper important work and personal relationships.
> ➤ Knowing when to "unhook" is a critical ability.
> ➤ Text with good judgment and with care.

CHAPTER 10

Using Social Media to Make—Not Break—Your Career

*I*n less than a decade, the explosion of social media has changed the way we present ourselves to the world. The phenomenon has brought a certain glamour to ordinary people's lives, as everyone who uses these resources achieves a bit of celebrity status, at least among their connections. Whereas we once shared information with friends and family through letters, phone calls, and later e-mails, today we can put our lives on display in sometimes extravagant detail. We can let hundreds of people know where we are having dinner, with whom we are dining, and the quality of the food. We can share vacation photos and pictures of our newborns minutes after birth. We can let our friends know that we just got a promotion or that we are looking for a job. And depending on how we set controls, friends of friends may also be in the know about what's going on in our lives.

We feel connected to our favorite athletes, recording artists, CEOs, news anchors, or senators by following them on Twitter and communicating with them—or with a community of strangers who want to weigh in on something the celebrity has said or done.

UNDERSTANDING SOCIAL MEDIA'S REWARDS AND RISKS

These amazing platforms have changed the way we live, and the fascination with them doesn't seem to be abating. We love the intimacy, even if it is artificial or contrived in some cases. However, we have all heard the horror stories and seen the results of social media gone wrong. We've discovered that private isn't total or forever, and the consequences go beyond simple embarrassment. Inappropriate use of social media can end careers—and important relationships.

Christopher Steiner and Helen Coster, writing for *Forbes*, cite numerous bizarre examples of social media disasters: a New York City med tech posting pictures of a murder victim; a Pennsylvania college professor asking if anyone knows a hit man; an Atlanta police officer leaking information about a case; a daughter whose father was fired going on an obscenity-laced rant on the company's website.

Employees who trash their employers, even on their personal pages, have found themselves quickly unemployed. Adhering to a few guidelines can keep you from getting into hot water and finding yourself out of a job or even the job market.

Understand the purpose of various social media resources. Decide which social media channels work best for you and your objectives. Do you primarily want to stay in touch with friends from college or your widespread family? Are you an incurable collector, planning a wedding, renovating a house that was a huge bargain, or collecting recipes? Are you building a network to help further your career? Do you want entrées into companies, both big and small? Are you a photo addict? Would you rather communicate with pictures than with words? Do you want to weigh in on major events? Or all of the above?

No matter what your preference may be, you can create an online presence to accommodate your preferences. Knowing the strengths and weaknesses of each medium, however, will keep you from using a less effective method for your purpose.

Some people use Facebook as a constant stream of thoughts throughout the day, when Twitter might be a better choice. Because information is so easy to share, it's also easy to misuse. Although most experts consider Facebook more informal and primarily geared to friends and family, businesses and groups can use it effectively, particularly to garner support or publicize events.

On the other hand, LinkedIn may not be the best site for describing your honeymoon. But it's a great place to build your network, through endorsements, congratulatory messages, and updated profiles. Likewise, Pinterest may not be the best place to look for a job unless you are interested in showing your decorating skills, renovation proficiency, or culinary acumen.

Understand your company's policy, best practices, and corporate culture. Remember that when you are at work, your company is paying for your time and you are usually using company-owned equipment.

Companies are also realizing that employees can damage the corporate brand by what they post on their own social media sites. According to Anthonia Akitunde, editor at Federated Media Publishing, Inc., a hamburger-chain employee in Japan posted to Instagram a photo of himself lying on a pile of burger buns. Infamous photos and videos of employees of a pizza company engaging in disgusting acts with food have gone viral, creating grief for the company's corporate communication departments and, at least temporarily, tarnishing the organization's brand.

According to the 2013 Professionalism in the Workplace study conducted by York College's Center for Professional Excellence, "Half of human resources professionals say that IT abuses have increased over the past five years among new college graduates."

For that reason, and as the number of employees who are sharing, liking, and tweeting grows incrementally, companies are beefing up their policies regarding employees' social media activities, particularly on the job. Make sure that you know exactly what your company encourages or allows and stay well inside the boundaries. Ignoring them is at one's on peril.

Use good judgment about posting photos. Unless you restrict your social media site to close friends and family, post a professional-looking profile picture. Your cat or a photo of when you were three years old may be cute, but you are wiser if you use an attractive head shot to present yourself to the world.

Avoid tagging friends in photos without their permission. And, certainly, refrain from posting photos of friends (or yourself for that matter) in questionable or compromising situations. Digital lifestyle expert Mario Armstrong and psychiatrist Janet Taylor warn about posting throwback photos of high school and college friends.

A photo of an upstanding father of five hammered at a fraternity party twenty-five years ago can create unnecessary angst and concern about who might see it—far beyond the momentary chuckle that it might produce.

Armstrong and Taylor discuss the proper etiquette parents should follow when posting photos of other people's children on social media. Do not post pictures of other people's children (say, at a birthday party) without every parent's written consent. Although this advice seems draconian, realize that once a photo is out there, it can go any-where—including porn sites—and, furthermore, it could fall into the hands of pedophiles. The enjoyment of easy access and widespread sharing is a double-edged sword, and the great fun and convenience also have a foreboding side.

Job seekers should make sure that their social media sites don't con-tain anything that might put off a potential employer. Don't assume that no one but your select "friends" can see your information. That hiring manager may be a friend of a friend.

Think long-term about what you post. It's tempting and oh-so-easy to put your immediate reactions on the Internet. Alison Lough-man, Web content coordinator at ASHRAE (American Society of Heating, Refrigerating and Air Conditioning Engineers), reminds us that "our thoughts can get distributed to thousands of people in sec-onds—and this can be dangerous." For example, telling too much about your habits or your whereabouts can perhaps give the wrong people access to you.

Furthermore, if you don't think before you post, that mistake can follow you for years. Dr. Lois Frankel, author of *Nice Girls Don't Get the Corner Office*, notes that trying to track down and remove ill-advised posts is like trying to put toothpaste back in the tube.

Before you vent or post something that is hilarious at the moment, think about how you would feel if you were on the receiving end of your communication, or how you might feel about your flash of bril-liance in a year—or when you are in a position of leadership.

We will continue to explore and exploit the ever-expanding fron-tiers of technology, but human decision-making, common sense, and respect for each other should always be your default setting.

THE BOTTOM LINE

- ➤ Understand the particular purpose and strengths of various social media platforms, and choose the ones that work best for you.
- ➤ Your online presence can reflect positively or negatively on your company's brand.

➤ Realize the risks of posting photos, particularly of children.

➤ Think long-term about your social media presence.

➤ Common sense and respect for others and for yourself should guide your decisions.

CHAPTER 11

Travel Courtesy

Don't Leave Home Without It

After a five-hour flight in a cramped seat, a ninety-minute layover turns into a four-hour delay. You're tired, hungry, and will never make that morning meeting if the flight is delayed any longer. The airport seats are uncomfortable and you're surrounded by irate passengers. To top it all off, you are looking at three days of wall-to-wall meetings and business lunches and dinners. You feel out of control and out of sorts. Let's face it; travel is not your favorite part of the job.

*S*tressful at best and traumatic at worst, business travel often brings out our evil twin. We become ruder, less tolerant, and shorter-fused than we would normally allow ourselves to be. Perhaps it's because we're tired and uneasy about being in unfamiliar territory. Or perhaps we think that because we're surrounded by people we'll likely never see again, it really doesn't matter how we behave.

KEEPING THE SKIES FRIENDLY

The majority of business travel today takes place on airplanes, which involves getting to the airport, negotiating our way through busy terminals, making it through security checks, and boarding planes that attempt to raise efficient use of space to an art form. In this arena of forced intimacy, it's important to not lose sight of the importance of good manners. Not only will this understanding help you avoid offending others, in the end it can also help you have a more enjoyable—or at least less stressful—trip, because your outward behavior will influence your outlook and disposition. In addition, it's likely that other people will behave more pleasantly toward you.

Most people who travel by air have two major complaints about their fellow passengers: people who carry too much luggage onto the plane or whose luggage is too large to be comfortably accommodated, and people who want to strike up a conversation that lasts from coast to coast. And, as airlines begin to allow use of smartphones in flight, the possibilities for irritating each other expand exponentially.

Here are some ways to minimize stress and make you a welcome travel companion.

Consider what you carry. There's no doubt about it: Unless you travel first-class, most airplanes provide relatively little room for baggage. Here are a few tips about carry-on baggage to make things easier on yourself as well as others:

➤ Make sure that you meet the size requirements; some airlines consider handbags part of the carry-on total.

➤ If you need to use a particular piece of carry-on luggage during the flight, remember to put it underneath your seat so that you won't have to open the bins en route and risk dumping a briefcase on another passenger's head.

➤ If you have a piece of rolling luggage, guide it carefully to avoid bumping the knees and elbows of people already seated.

➤ Lend a hand if you see someone struggling with a bulky item.

Know when and how to end a conversation. In most cases, we can't choose our seatmates in public transportation, and the issue of conversation frequently arises. Handling the situation with tact can pose a challenge, but enduring an unwanted situation can make that portion of your trip miserable.

If you're seated next to chatty Kathy and you don't feel like talking, politely tell the person that you have to get some work done, you need to get some sleep, or you just can't wait to see how the novel you're reading ends. If the person has nothing to read, offer a paper or recommend an article in the airline magazine.

Remember, however, that some people talk from nervousness or outright fear of flying. If you suspect that this might be the case, take a few minutes to lend a bit of emotional support.

If you are the one who starts the conversation, be sensitive to signals that your seatmate doesn't want to talk. One-word answers to your questions, little eye contact, or an active computer or tablet screen, for example, should serve as hints that you shouldn't pursue the discussion.

Avoid typical annoyances. Even small distractions may irritate people during the hours you're together in close quarters. Look behind you before reclining your seat. If you chew gum, do it quietly. Use good table manners if you are on a flight that involves a meal. And go easy on the perfume or aftershave or, better still, don't use it. Many people are allergic to the ingredients and may, consequently, arrive at their destination with a splitting headache.

Don't let your children be a nuisance. We often have blind spots about our children and may not realize that others may not find them as delightful as we do. If your children are old enough to understand, talk to them before the trip about travel behavior and enforce rules during the journey. If they are small, bring things to entertain them, and if they have a tantrum, ask the flight attendant if you can take the child to the back of the plane until the situation is calmer. It should go without saying that you shouldn't allow your children to kick or bump the back of the chair in front of them, although amazingly, many travelers don't seem to be aware of how irritating such behaviors can be.

Respect airline personnel. A lot of people work hard to make your trip as comfortable as possible. It's good manners to let these hardworking people know that we appreciate them by thanking them for their efforts. If a particular flight attendant has been especially helpful during your flight, mention it to the head flight attendant when you are deplaning.

ONCE YOU LAND: COURTESY AT HOME OR ABROAD

As the world becomes increasingly smaller, business travel is as likely to mean a trip to Paris, France as Paris, Texas. When traveling abroad, keep some basic rules in mind.

TIPS ON TIPPING

When it's appropriate, show your appreciation with a tip. While there are no hard-and-fast rules for how much to tip while traveling, here are some guidelines:

Airport baggage handlers: $1.00 a bag
Hotel bellhops: $1.00/bag (an additional $1.00/bag to the person who brings your bags into the hotel lobby if different from the person who takes you to your room)
Hotel doorman: $1.00 for hailing a cab
Housekeeper: $1.00 for delivering a requested item to your room and $1.00-to $3.00/day for cleaning your room
Bathroom attendant: $0.50 to $1.00
Valet: $1.00 minimum for both the person who takes your car and the one who delivers it back to you

The Gracious Colleague

Remember that courtesy also applies to coworkers who are traveling with you. If you're traveling with others from your company, don't let the normal stress of travel cause you to neglect courteous behavior toward them. And just because you are out of town, don't assume that the workday extends beyond normal business hours. Allow your colleagues the option of having some downtime. And if you are the one who needs some time alone, you should feel comfortable politely declining the invitation to "make a night of it."

If you need to work in the evening and need your colleagues to join you, show them the same good manners that you would if you were on your home turf. Give them a choice, if possible, and if they have no choice, explain the need for the extra hours.

The Gracious Guest

When you arrive at your business destination, make yourself a welcome guest to your clients and customers by following some basic rules of conduct. Remember that you represent your firm, so your social behavior can have as much impact as your carefully planned presentation. Even if you choose not to mix business with pleasure, such as by extending the workday with drinks or dinner, being gracious in your interaction with others will leave them feeling positive about your visit.

Follow up with a thank-you note or gift. A thank-you note is always appropriate, even if your experience was entirely business, without a social dimension. Businesspeople usually accommodate your schedule by adjusting their own while you are on-site, so acknowledging their hospitality can make them feel good about the experience.

If you are entertained while traveling and wish to say thanks with a gift, you are often safe with flowers. Around the globe, however, types and colors of flowers have different meanings. For example, according to Terri Morrison and Wayne Conaway in *Kiss, Bow, or Shake Hands,* in Germany, one should always give bouquets of uneven-numbered flowers (except thirteen) and avoid red roses, which are reserved for courting, and certain lilies that are used for funerals. Check with a local florist for a suitable selection. Chocolates are also a widely accepted thank-you gift. If your company has attractive promotional gifts, people often appreciate a token of your appreciation and a souvenir from your organization.

When in Rome

Today we're lucky that we can know a lot more about the rest of the world than we once did. Bookstores are filled with excellent resources to help us as we venture abroad. Make use of these resources. Learn something about the culture and customs of the region you will be traveling to. At the most basic level, learn the appropriate use of handshakes, eye contact, and other gestures, as traditions vary widely around the globe. Learn a few words of that country's language, particularly the phrase "thank you." And remember that a smile is almost universally positive in human interaction.

Show respect for the country or region you're visiting. When you are visiting another city, state, or country, remember that this is home to the people around you. Express admiration and appreciation for the surroundings and avoid criticism, even if you aren't crazy about the place or it is very different from your home turf. Complaining about the cold in Buffalo, the traffic in L.A., or Southwestern food in Tucson isn't going to endear you to the natives. And never make a joke about the place or the people.

Demonstrate an appreciation for the city and the region. Develop an admiration for the history of the area you are visiting, and show interest by asking questions about it. For example, know how to pronounce the name correctly. Not long ago, when I was on a trip to teach a workshop in Reno, a woman approached me at the end of my presentation to thank me for pronouncing "Nevada" correctly. Fortunately, I had asked a hotel employee about the correct pronunciation that morning.

Dress conservatively. Whenever you travel, particularly if you are alone, avoid calling unnecessary attention to yourself. Although throughout the United States most people are tolerant of expressive attire, hairstyles, and makeup, other cultures may not be so receptive. Both women and men should dress conservatively and modestly and limit the amount of jewelry they wear. Before a trip women, in particular, should check to see if they should avoid wearing certain items of clothing. For example, are pantsuits acceptable for female business travelers in a specific country?

Someone once said that you should treat everyone as though you were going to have to spend the rest of your life with that person in a very small room. Particularly when we're traveling, a little consideration can go a long way toward taking some of the bumps out of the road.

THE BOTTOM LINE

- ➤ Stressful at best and traumatic at worst, traveling often causes us to be ruder, more intolerant, and shorter-fused than we are at home, perhaps because we think we will never see those people again.
- ➤ Keep the skies friendly by being particularly courteous in close quarters.
- ➤ Don't forget the people who make the process easier for you.
- ➤ Remember that courtesy on the road should apply to your traveling companions as well.
- ➤ Be a gracious guest wherever you travel.

PART 2

Best Behaviors at Work: Interacting with Bosses and Peers

CHAPTER 12

Terror on Both Sides of the Desk

Relieving Interview Stress

*J*ob searches can be nerve-racking, and the stress often only increases when it comes time to face an interviewer (or a panel of interviewers) and put our best foot forward. Facing anyone we're meeting for the first time and convincing that person that we are the answer to an organization's hiring need is a daunting task. Yet often the person conducting the interview is just as uncomfortable as the interviewee because he or she doesn't want to make a mistake that will affect the company.

Although for many people the interview process is the most dreaded part of the job search, it doesn't have to be. With the right amount of preparation and a realistic perspective, the job interview, handled with professionalism and finesse, can be the key to your success. And if you happen to be the person on the interviewer's side of the desk, you can boost your hiring success by mastering some simple techniques.

Needless to say, both parties are under considerable pressure during an interview, and certainly each party has an agenda. Even so, the interviewee and the interviewer have clear responsibilities to each other, and failing to acknowledge and fulfill those obligations can leave a lasting negative impression.

GUIDELINES FOR THE INTERVIEWEE

A job interview doesn't have to an unpleasant experience. With preparation and the right outlook, you can differentiate yourself favorably from the other candidates. Here are some guidelines to help you turn your next interview into the event that tips the decision in your favor.

Learn about the hiring company. Even though you are immersed in the job search, perhaps to the point of obsessing over it, remember that this process isn't all about you. A company has a lot at stake when it makes someone an offer, and hiring managers are looking for ways to differentiate between the satisfactory and the excellent.

Ken Lee, Graduate Career Counselor at Georgia State University's Robinson College of Business, says that you should also do research, if possible, on the person with whom you will be meeting. Ask for the name of your interviewer and see if you can find information about this

INTERVIEWEE CHECKLIST

- ➤ Clearly written directions to interview location
- ➤ Contact phone number, in case you're delayed
- ➤ Pad for taking notes
- ➤ Questions for interviewer, about the company and the job
- ➤ Fifty-word response for "Tell me about yourself"
- ➤ Collapsible umbrella that will fit in a briefcase (in case of an unexpected shower)
- ➤ High-quality pen for taking notes
- ➤ Breath mints
- ➤ Headache medicine
- ➤ Handkerchief or facial tissue
- ➤ Extra necktie for men/additional pair of pantyhose for women (in case of spills or snags)
- ➤ Neatly pressed clothing and shined shoes
- ➤ Professional and businesslike hairstyle
- ➤ Combination briefcase/handbag for women (so that you aren't carrying two objects)
- ➤ No rings on right hand in case of a bone-crusher handshake from the interviewer
- ➤ Newspaper to catch up on the day's events to use in interview conversation

individual on the company website or on the person's social media profiles. Knowing something about that person can help you relate more effectively.

Rather than spending all your energy reading one of those "perfect answer for every interview question" books, do some research on the company and its industry. If the company has recently been recognized for some achievement, be prepared to talk about it. If the firm faces challenges, some questions about its current strategies will show that you don't have unrealistic expectations.

Be prepared to ask questions. Asking insightful questions not only positions you as a thoughtful candidate but also gives you more control of the meeting. However, you need to ask questions that reveal some of your abilities and interests as well as your desire to know more about the workings of the organization.

Make sure that some of your questions touch on how you can contribute to the firm's success if you get the job and what criteria are in place to define outstanding performance. Avoid questions that seem self-serving, such as the number of vacation days during the first year or the robustness of the benefits package.

Don't misrepresent your abilities or experience. Although you want to appear in the most favorable light, resist the temptation, both in your resume and in your interview, to misrepresent your accomplishments. Even stretching the truth can have dire consequences. Did you lead the project or were you a support person? What were your specific duties on the team? Many people have assumed that no one would ever check their resume or their assertions, and they found out the hard way that their assumption was a big mistake.

Being honest is not only the right thing to do but it also keeps you from setting unrealistic expectations for your future performance.

Be prepared for the unexpected. An interview is an appointment that needs to go off without a hitch. Yet we're all familiar with Murphy's Law. Try to anticipate the worst and prepare for it. First of all, get on your way in plenty of time to arrive early. Being late for a job interview is generally an unforgivable faux pas. Not only does it inconvenience others, but, according Louis Imundo, author of *The Effective Supervisor's Handbook,* lateness may even indicate a potential problem with authority.

THINGS NOT TO SAY ON A JOB INTERVIEW: THE FORMIDABLE FIVE MISTAKES

1. **Don't badmouth your former company or your boss.** Your former boss may have made Attila the Hun look like Mr. Rogers, but bashing that person will make you look like a whiner. If you were part of a large layoff or restructuring, be honest, but avoid coming across as a victim.

2. **Don't ask about company's benefits, vacation days, or sick days, or request special hours.** One of the biggest turnoffs to an interviewer is a potential hire who seems more interested in company benefits and time off than in the job itself.

3. **Don't get caught without a good reason for why you want *this* job.** "It looks like an easy (or fun) job" won't win you any points. Saying "I just need a job" or "I'm looking for something to tide me over until I get accepted to graduate school" won't inspire anyone to hire you, either.

4. **Don't ask a question about something that's prominent on the company's website.** "So, what do you guys do?" will indicate that you haven't done your homework. Even though you are immersed in the job search perhaps to the point of obsessing over it, remember that this process isn't all about you. A company has a lot at stake when it makes someone an offer.

5. **Don't make your interviewer your adversary.** Avoid coming on too strong with statements such as "I want your job." That kind of aggressive interviewing had its day for a while, but most executives are looking for a reasonable blend of confidence and humility. And in many companies today, collaboration is the watchword.

Traffic and transportation schedules, however, can create delays beyond your control, so your cell phone is essential if you aren't going to be there on time. Make sure that your phone is fully charged and have all the contact information for your appointment with you so that you have the number easily at hand. Most people will try to accommodate you if extenuating circumstances interfere with your arrival and if they have some notice.

Unless the sky is cloudless, carry with you clean, pressed rain gear and a working umbrella with all the spines intact. You don't want to arrive at your meeting after getting drenched in a rainstorm.

Bring something to read or work on in case you have to wait. Although some interviewers will make interviewees wait to see how they deal with the inconvenience, in many instances company emergencies may keep an interviewer from being on time. If you can be productive while you wait, you won't run the risk of appearing impatient or agitated when you actually get into the meeting. In the event that you actually have to reschedule because of an extended emergency, accept the change in plans graciously and with good humor.

Remember that first impressions are critical. Look sharp. Savvy interviewers know that most people showing up for a job interview are presenting their best professional appearance, probably looking better than they will ever look in the workplace. So go all out to create that great first response from your interviewer. Wear an outfit that fits well and is clean and pressed. Choose something professional and conservative; save your flashy fashions for another time. And don't forget your shoes. Make sure they are clean, polished, and conservative. Finally, if you need a haircut, get a good one.

Relax and project confidence. A good interviewer pays attention to the little things that give clues to a candidate's character: the way you walk into a room, how you shake hands, and if you make strong eye contact. Even though you may feel nervous, which is natural, be confident in yourself and your abilities. Visualize yourself walking into the interview room with poise, looking the interviewer in the eye, and shaking hands with a firm grip. Remember that you've worked hard to get where you are, and you should feel good about yourself. That confidence will translate to a favorable first impression.

Treat everyone you meet with respect. Don't save your good manners for when you walk into the interviewer's office. You never know who might provide the good word that gives you the advantage over the competition. One executive I know always used his secretary as a barometer for assessing candidates. After an interview, he would always head over to see her and ask, "What do you think?" If the applicant had been curt, disrespectful, or generally ignored her, that person didn't get hired. Obviously, candidates never knew that they were being tested in the reception area. Therefore, if they were genuinely courteous to other staff members, the executive could feel pretty confident they would also be courteous on the job.

Always send a thank-you note. Although a handwritten note is preferable, at the very least send a thank-you e-mail. The sooner you write it the more sincere it will be and the more someone will appreciate your quick response. Writing the note within twenty-four hours will allow you to capture the enthusiasm that the interview generated. However, if you have delayed in writing the note, do not assume that it's too late. Sending the note late is far better than not at all.

In your note, mention some specifics of the visit, so your note doesn't sound like a form letter. Even some of the social aspects of the visit can be appropriate for inclusion. For example, "Thanks so much for recommending that great Brazilian restaurant. I'm going to try it this weekend."

Since you will probably be sending the note before you know the outcome of the interview, you might also want to restate your interest in the position and your anticipation about the possibility of employment. On the other hand, if the interview has convinced you that you don't want to work there, be gracious in thanking the interviewer for the opportunity to meet, without elaborating on your desire, or lack thereof, to work for that organization.

GUIDELINES FOR THE INTERVIEWER

When conducting an interview, you can boost your hiring effectiveness by adhering to some basic principles.

Create an atmosphere of comfort and security. Unless the job requires a "stress" interview, you need to create an atmosphere that alleviates an already nerve-racking situation, for you and for the interviewee. When you greet the applicant, help put him or her at ease by making rapport-building small talk. Ask if the candidate had trouble finding the location, make a remark about the weather, or chat about any other neutral, non-job-related topic. Offer the interviewee a soft drink, coffee, or water; if he or she accepts the offer for refreshment, you should have something, too. Arrange a private setting for the interview so that you won't be subject to interruptions and can concentrate and help put the applicant at ease.

Once settled in the interview room, spend some more time building rapport by asking questions about the person's interests and providing an overview of how the interview will proceed.

INTERVIEWER CHECKLIST

➤ Confirmation of room reservation if conducting the interview in a conference room

➤ Message left with key contacts that you are unavailable until a specific time

➤ Business cards

➤ Refreshment setup, if appropriate

➤ Pen and pad for taking notes

➤ Breath mints

➤ Attire reflecting company standards, even for an after-hours or weekend interview

➤ Clear job description for the position

➤ Notes on the few essential attributes needed for success in this job

➤ Applicant's resume and background information

➤ List of what you need to clarify, verify, or explore in greater detail

➤ Prepared questions you must ask

➤ List of illegal questions you may not ask

➤ Authorization to offer job and salary, or else knowledge of next steps to communicate to candidate

Be prepared for the interview. Although you may have an extremely full schedule, remember that the interview is important both for the applicant and the company. If you look at the candidate's application for the first time when he or she sits down for the interview, you are shortchanging everyone.

In addition to familiarizing yourself with information about the applicant, you need to structure the interview carefully and be able to communicate that structure to the candidate. You might say something like, "Michael, I'm going to discuss the major responsibilities of the job, and then I want to go over the last couple of assignments you listed on your resume. I'm interested in how you performed your duties and what resources were at your disposal. Then I would like to take some questions from you. And, finally, we'll talk more about the job in additional detail and outline where we go from here."

Anticipate any questions the person may have, about the company, about the job, even about the job that you currently hold. You expect the applicant to come to the interview with thoughtful questions, and you need to be prepared to give succinct and clear answers.

Listen attentively. Part of building rapport, and for that matter being a good interviewer, involves listening attentively and actively. The ability to listen is critical to making good decisions. Experts tell us one of the biggest mistakes interviewers make is talking too much during the interview. Consultant Pat MacMillan, CEO of Triaxia Partners and author of the book *Hiring Excellence*, suggests that ideally, the interviewer should talk about 20 percent of the time and the applicant 80 percent. Asking a perfunctory question and then pondering your next question instead of listening to the answer will quickly make the interviewee uncomfortable, giving the impression that you are not particularly interested in what he or she has to say. Furthermore, you will miss the opportunity to learn valuable information about the person— not only from verbal answers, but from nonverbal cues as well. You want to be alert to what the potential employee either *doesn't* say or is superficial or vague about in answering your questions.

Be honest. Are you the hiring manager or the screener? Will you make the decision or will subsequent interviews take place? Are you interviewing a large number of candidates? Does the job in question offer opportunity for growth or is it a long-term assignment performing the same function? Is the company enjoying great prosperity and expansion, or is cost-cutting a big deal? Be honest in answering these and any other questions the interviewee has about the position and his or her prospective role with the company.

Beginning any relationship, whether professional or personal, based on anything less than honesty is a recipe for disaster. If the person you hire discovers that you lied or exaggerated about the job, the company, or your roles and responsibilities, your credibility is shot—perhaps permanently, and the company itself may even be put in an unfavorable light. If the position turns out to be significantly different from what the interviewee had been led to believe it would be, chances are you will have a dissatisfied employee on your staff, perhaps forcing you to start the whole process over again before too long.

Clarify the next steps. The interview has come to an end. Now what? Obviously, you thank the applicant for coming and sharing important information openly. Now the applicant wants to know what can he or she should expect next, and when.

Have a clear plan for the next phase of the process. When will you make the decision? Will you call the applicant for follow-up interviews? How soon can you let the person know whether the process stops here or moves forward?

Make sure that you share this information with the candidate and be open to answering any further questions about the process. The applicant should leave knowing when he or she will have either a final answer or a subsequent meeting. Finally, be sure to follow up in the manner you described. Don't tell the interviewee to expect to hear back from you within a week only to be left in the dark for three weeks.

Follow up. After the interview, if you don't feel that you have the time or focus to handle the follow-up yourself, enlist someone from human resources or an assistant to contact all of the candidates (either by phone or in writing) and apprise them of the status of the process. Don't put off breaking the bad news if the answer is negative. The sooner you provide closure on your company's relationship with this person, the sooner the applicant can focus on looking elsewhere. If you want to proceed further with the candidate, the earlier you can communicate this message the higher the likelihood that the candidate will still be available and interested.

Many job applicants can relate horror stories about the insensitive or downright rude treatment they received from companies to which they have applied. A woman working on a graduate degree in computer information systems tells of problems with her interview process at one company. "I'm currently on my ninth interview with this firm," she lamented, "and they make no effort to keep me in the loop. Even the human resources manager, whose job it is to maintain contact with candidates, never lets me know the status of the process. I have to initiate all communication, and it always takes more than one attempt."

In another situation, a financial analyst had what he thought was a great interview, yet it took four messages and three e-mails over the course of a month before he heard anything about the company's decision.

Whether you're interested in the candidate or not, it's your responsibility to communicate the decision. Be courteous and considerate, and don't force the candidate to call repeatedly to find out what happened.

ON EITHER SIDE OF THE DESK

Dr. Martin Luther King, Jr. once said, "The ultimate measure of a man is not where he stands in moments of comfort, but where he stands at times of challenge and controversy." Job interviews don't qualify as "moments of comfort" for either party, but they can be great learning experiences as well as opportunities to make fruitful connections. Even if the job isn't a fit, you never know when you might cross paths with that person again. If you have used the situation advantageously, your efforts may be rewarded in ways you did not expect.

THE BOTTOM LINE

- ➤ The interview process can be rewarding if it is approached with the right attitude.
- ➤ Preparation on both sides is critical to a successful interview.
- ➤ Both the interviewer and the interviewee have clear social and professional responsibilities to each other.
- ➤ Follow-up is a critical step in the process, from both perspectives.

CHAPTER 13

The New Job

Getting Started on the Right Foot

*I*n today's workplace, people are leaving companies, either volun-
tarily or through mergers, downsizing, or termination, and joining
new ones in record numbers. Gone are the days when a person spent a
lifetime with the same company. Starting over, moving up, and making
strategic career moves have become the norm.

When you're starting a new job, no matter how thoroughly you
have researched the company or how sure you are that the job is perfect for you, actually starting work in that new organization feels a lot
like the first day at a new school. You're the new kid on the block, and
your established colleagues will be sizing you up to see how well you're
going to fit in. You're hoping to make a good impression and to be
accepted in and well suited for your new environment.

The reality is that no matter how sure you are during the interview
process that you want the job, when you actually report to work, you'll
likely experience some reservations. You may find yourself asking,
"Have I done the right thing? Is this company the best place for me?"
Furthermore, although most companies go to a lot of trouble to recruit
candidates, many come up short when it comes to bringing new hires
on board effectively. Rather than making sure that they create a climate of trust and an environment for growth, managers and coworkers
often leave it up to new staff members to fend for themselves in carv-
ing out a niche in the department or company.

PLAN FOR SUCCESS IN A NEW POSITION

When you start a new job or even transfer to another position within
your own company, you and your new manager have about sixty days

to decide whether you fit in. A few tips may make the process easier and help ensure your success.

Don't be a know-it-all. Though it may be a cliché, you really *do* have only one chance to make a first impression. As you're making that critical initial impact, choose your words and actions wisely. Although you certainly want to do some positive image building, don't exaggerate. Yes, you're a whiz with a computer. No, you're not the next Steve Jobs.

Also, you would be wise to avoid making off-the-cuff statements that may come back to haunt you. "I just needed a job to hold me over until I get accepted to grad school" isn't the best way to endear yourself to those who have spent time and money hiring you. A remark such as "I wanted to try retailing to see if I like it" may show up on a performance review to demonstrate your lack of commitment. Resist the impulse to make comparisons to your old company or position, too. Avoid statements such as, "When I was with ABC, we did it this way." Be open to learning how your new company does things. If you see opportunities to share some valuable insights, find an appropriate time to do so after you've settled into the job.

Take the initiative and be friendly. Don't wait for people to come to you. Trying to meet as many people as possible during the first few days will establish you as a friendly person who wants to be part of the team and who takes charge of a situation.

Shaking hands, listening carefully for people's names, and mentioning what you will be doing with the company shows that you are making an effort to relate and get on board quickly. Even if you don't remember everyone's name, you will have demonstrated that you're interested in people as individuals.

Avoid instant "friendships." That coworker who wants to take you under his or her wing may be a genuinely nice person who just wants you to feel at home in your new surroundings. *Or* the person may simply want to take advantage of what seems your vulnerable position. Worse yet, an office feud may be raging, and an employee wants to win you over before the other side enlists you. If you encounter a colleague who is too eager to dish the dirt on everyone in the department, you will do well to keep the relationship at arm's length. Don't get tangled in this kind of behavior, and remember that someone who is eager to badmouth someone to you is probably just as likely to make you the target of tongue wagging.

Even if a friendly person has pure motives, it's a good idea not to lock yourself into a particular network when you are new on the job. Allow time for working relationships and friendships to develop naturally, based on mutual goals and interests.

Build a support network. If possible, search out a mentor in the new firm, even if you have to ask HR or your manager to suggest someone. A person who is outside your area of day-to-day-responsibilities can be a huge asset in helping you to see the big picture as it pertains to the company. You will help yourself and impress others if you understand the company's strategic initiatives and how your job contributes to corporate goals.

With or without a mentor, get to know people who can tell you what you need to know to succeed—teammates, project leaders, or support staff.

Earn a reputation as a team player. Look for ways to help others who may be overwhelmed with work at the moment. When the time comes that you need a little extra help, you'll find colleagues willing to pitch in. Also, seek opportunities to praise those who have been helpful to you. Laurie and Bob Rozakis, authors of *The Complete Idiot's Guide to Office Politics,* suggest using the office grapevine to share anecdotes about the accomplishments and kindnesses of others. It won't take long for the word to get back to the person who helped you that you really appreciated it and that you were willing to give credit where it's due. Keep the praise light and casual, however. Laying it on too thick makes you come across as phony.

Ask questions and solicit feedback. Within the first month, have a "How am I doing?" meeting with the boss. It's dangerous to assume that you're doing what the company expects. Jim Webb, a retired human resources manager for Procter & Gamble, says, "If you want to fit in fast, and succeed in the process, be open to learning as much as you can. Don't be afraid to look like you don't know something. Be willing to take risks and ask meaningful questions, because you will learn a lot faster that way." In fact, Webb adds, "the inability to ask a question is the most significant sign of insecurity."

Webb also points out that the first few weeks on a job are a great time to do a lot of listening. Companies are always assessing employees' listening skills. Being a good listener not only positions you as a person interested in others' knowledge and opinions, but also enables you to pick up on the speaker's unspoken feelings.

For example, if Eleanor's body language becomes negative and she adopts a sarcastic tone when she talks about a particular vendor, you may make a mental note to be a bit cautious in your initial dealings with that person. Give yourself some time to decide how to approach that vendor. You may decide to keep your interaction neutral and guarded until you have a chance to know more and form your own opinions.

Get to know the corporate culture. Is the company one big family, or does everyone come into work, do a job, and then go separate ways? Does the organization value teamwork or individual performance? Is the atmosphere relaxed and informal or more intense? Do some research on the "face" the company presents to the public. Can you find articles that discuss the organization's reputation? Learn quickly about the company's inside jokes, rituals, pet slogans, and values. What are the company's communication patterns? Top down? Impersonal? Open?

Even the physical layout of the office says something about the company's values and motives. I once coached a manager who worked for a company in which all offices had glass walls and no doors. For private conversations, a couple of small conference rooms were the only options. The company had chosen to make a clear architectural statement that everyone in the firm had access to both people and information. The faster you pick up on the culture's distinguishing features, the quicker you will become integrated into the new organization.

Starting a new job is a lot like setting out on a journey. Preparation, focus, and awareness of our surroundings once we're on the way can go a long way toward preventing a disastrous wrong turn that leads to a dead end.

THE BOTTOM LINE

- ➤ Job turnover is much more common today than at any other time in American corporate history.
- ➤ Assume that you and your new manager have about sixty days to decide whether you fit in.
- ➤ Don't be afraid to ask for feedback.
- ➤ Build alliances by being a team player who gives credit where it's due.
- ➤ Build a support network that may or may not include a mentor.
- ➤ Identify the characteristics of the corporate culture.

CHAPTER 14

Office Space

Make Working Together More Enjoyable and Productive

*W*e can all enjoy the antics of Dilbert and the long-suffering, cubicle-bound workers in those cartoons. Yet it's not quite so funny when what the cartoon characters endure happens to us.

The open office lined with cubicles rather than rooms with doors has cut costs and made the workplace more efficient. The idea emerged from a combination of the move to reengineer organizations with fewer command-and-control managers and the theory that collaboration among peers, even among those in different departments, would improve effectiveness and communication. However, an open floor plan has significant drawbacks. When you're trying to concentrate on a major project, laughter, loud talking, general noise, or the smell of pizza in the next cubicle or down the hall in the break room can really interfere with your concentration and test your patience.

THE CONSIDERATE COLLEAGUE

Good manners should extend to all areas of the workplace to make the office environment more conducive to work and to reduce unnecessary stress. Generally, some small behavioral adjustments can make a huge difference between conflict and congeniality.

Do a reality check on your workplace behaviors. Think about all the habits of coworkers that annoy you. Have you ever worked with someone with a laugh that was just a little too hearty or who spoke in such a loud voice that every conversation he had near your office meant a disruption for you? Irritating behaviors in the workplace are probably not difficult to list.

Now think about your own actions and behavior. Are you guilty of any conduct at work that might irritate or disturb your coworkers? Do you have a tendency toward carrying on phone conversations loud enough to keep everyone around you informed of your business (and even personal) affairs? Do you hold hallway conversations outside other people's offices? Taking stock of your own performance can help you make sure you are not guilty of any inconsiderate workplace habits.

Keep your workspace tidy and professional. Your cubicle or office sends a message about you and your professionalism. No one expects a busy professional's office to be spotless and organized at all times; however, the opposite extreme is not acceptable, either. Colleagues and visitors coming in to your office should not get the impression that you are hopelessly disorganized or downright sloppy, nor should they fear for their own safety trying to navigate the obstacle course from your cubicle or office entrance to the nearest chair. Regularly take time—at the end of each workday or the end of the week—to put things in order. Not only will you improve your image, but you will also increase your productivity.

Furthermore, if you choose to bedeck your workspace with some personal items—photographs, art, or mementos of any kind—keep it low key and in good taste. Make sure that the things you choose don't offend someone else. Off-color or perverse humor and slogans, as well as pictures, calendars, posters, or cartoons that could insult or embarrass others, have no place at work.

Practice healthy hygiene. Everyone admires a responsible and dedicated worker, but if you're sick and sneezing all day long, your coworkers would probably prefer that you were a little less conscientious and used a sick day or two instead. Don't risk making everyone else ill just because you'd rather not call in sick. If you only have a mild cough or cold, or even a noncontagious allergy, remember to cover your mouth when you cough or sneeze and dispose of used tissues.

Leave the microwave fish sticks at home. Smelly food is a close second to noise among primary cubicle offenses. Although many companies provide employees with break rooms or pantries that include refrigerators and microwaves, this convenience doesn't mean that you should make yourself completely at home. When you pack food to reheat at work or to snack on in your cubicle, remember that what smells yummy to you might be an unpleasant odor to someone else.

I asked a marketing manager of a food-service chain to identify her number one cubicle vexation. Without hesitation she tagged "food odors" as the primary offender. Although what we eat is certainly a personal choice, your choice shouldn't impinge on other people's comfort. You can eat whatever you choose in the company cafeteria, a neighborhood restaurant, your own home, or on a park bench, but when choosing what to eat in the office, limit your choices to mild or odorless foods.

Avoid other olfactory offenders. A close second to food in the odor-complaint department is the excessive use of cologne or perfume. Even more serious than someone's simply not sharing your enthusiasm for a particular aroma, the reality is that many people are allergic to the chemicals or natural ingredients in these products. Negative reactions can include headaches, nausea, and sinus problems. A growing number of people have claimed to suffer even more severe reactions to perfumes and scented toiletries. The condition, known as multiple chemical sensitivities (MCS), can cause a wide range of debilitating physical reactions, prompting some companies and organizations to implement fragrance-free environments.

Even if your company has not reacted quite that aggressively, common courtesy dictates that no perfume (or a very light application) in the workplace and unscented personal care products are the best choice.

Don't be a noisy neighbor. For some people, noise rates as a more serious workplace offender than odors. If you like music while you work, consider headphones. When you need to talk with a coworker, go to that person's cubicle or office or use the telephone rather than shouting across the divide. If you need to get more than two people together for an impromptu meeting, find a small conference room or check with your neighbors before you have a meeting in your workspace to make sure the noise won't disrupt their work.

For the same reason, answer your phone promptly when you receive a call or set it to go into voice mail after only a few rings; also limit your use of the speakerphone. Many companies set aside rooms for conference calls. If yours does, make use of it. It's disruptive enough for people to have to hear *your* end of the conversation.

Place your cell phone ringer volume on low, with a ring that signals you with either a simple ring or a beep, or set the phone on vibrate. Be sure to take the phone with you or turn it off when you're leaving your office for an extended period of time. Again, forward calls to voice mail after only a few rings.

Don't expose your coworkers to your personal problems. Another common workplace complaint, especially by cubicle dwellers, involves neighbors who carry on personal or even intimate conversations without regard for who can overhear them. We all have issues and family emergencies, but other people don't need to be subjected to our private lives or our crises unless we want them to be involved. Keep personal conversations in the cube as neutral and inoffensive as possible, and always keep your voice low. Don't burden your coworkers with information they don't want to know (and you don't want to share with them). If you wouldn't be comfortable having a particular conversation while a coworker is sitting in the cube with you, why do it when the coworker is just behind a screen? Make your personal calls in a place where you have some privacy.

Remember that a cubicle is someone's office and respect others' spaces. Although foam and fabric half walls without doors don't look like traditional offices, cubicles are still "private" spaces, and the people working in them should be spared unwelcome intrusion. Since workers who still have traditional offices typically leave their office doors open, treat a cubicle the way you would an office with a door. That means don't walk into the cube (or an office for that matter) when someone is on the phone. If a coworker you need to speak with is on the phone, slip a note on his or her desk, explaining that you need a moment to discuss something, and then exit. In some cases, you may e-mail the person a message that you need to talk.

If someone looks busy, assume their "door" is closed. By the same token, if you don't want to be interrupted, avoid making eye contact with someone hovering around your door. Or you might say, "Is there something I can help you with quickly? I'm on a deadline, but I can answer a question."

If your cubicle or office directly faces a coworker's space, avoid staring into the cube or office.

If you overhear a conversation, even if it's a business-related issue that you feel the need to weigh in on, it is still presumptuous to comment about what you heard. What should you do, for example, if you hear a coworker speak rudely to a customer or agree to do something that is against company policy? Of course, people working in cubicles should know that others can hear their conversations, but unless what you heard is an especially serious matter or one involving company security, think carefully before confronting the person or reporting the conversation. If you have overheard something that is incorrect, unprofessional, or can result in harm to the company or its employees, you must react. Start by talking with the coworker directly, but be prepared to escalate the issue if your colleague's reaction is less than responsive to the problem.

Obviously, if the conversation you overheard is personal, pretend you never heard it, and by no means repeat it.

TIPS FOR BEING A GOOD OFFICE CITIZEN

- ➤ Put it back where it belongs.
- ➤ Indicate a reorder if you use the last of anything.
- ➤ Start the next pot of coffee if you pour the last cup.
- ➤ Refill the paper tray in the copier and return the machine to "normal" if you alter the setting.
- ➤ Keep things tidy.
- ➤ Don't overdo togetherness. Some cubicle "neighbors" time their lunch hours to allow everyone some private time.
- ➤ Consider real or artificial plants (company policy permitting) on your cube's partition to buffer noise.
- ➤ Use humor as a pleasant reprieve from the grind for everyone, but don't make coworkers the brunt of the joke.
- ➤ Pitch in and help out if necessary. Rather than a "my job/your job" mentality, think of what you do as "my part of our job."

A TEAM APPROACH TO A HARMONIOUS WORKPLACE

The workplace has, for many people, replaced the small communities and neighborhoods that generations before ours were accustomed to. With our coworkers we experience the highs and lows of personal and organizational successes and failures; we celebrate good times and survive crises. All of the emotions and frustrations of ordinary life are part and parcel of today's businesses.

Even though today's work environment is superior in many ways to that of our predecessors, in many instances the stress level is higher and the pace is more frantic. The more each of us can do to make our workplace a pleasant place to gather, interact, create, and achieve, the better for all of us as individuals and as organizations.

THE BOTTOM LINE

> ➤ Open offices featuring cubicles rather than offices with doors have cut costs and made the workplace more efficient.

> ➤ Some small behavioral adjustments can make the difference between congeniality and conflict.

> ➤ Check your own workplace behaviors to avoid annoying coworkers unnecessarily.

> ➤ A smell that is pleasing to you may not be so enjoyable to others. Avoid pungent foods and strong perfumes.

> ➤ Noise pollution—from loud phone conversations, ringing phones, music, and chitchat among coworkers—is a common workplace complaint.

> ➤ If you wouldn't have a particular conversation while a colleague was in your cubicle, don't have it if someone is in a nearby cubicle. Chances are your conversation can still be overheard.

> ➤ Treat cubicles like what they are—coworkers' offices.

> ➤ Good manners should extend throughout the workplace to make an office environment more enjoyable and to reduce stress.

CHAPTER 15

Getting Along with Your Manager

Spotting and Solving Personality Problems

You worked hard to develop the skills to do your job. You've found a position that allows you to put your training to good use. Things couldn't be more perfect. Now, six months into your employment, your dream job has turned into a surreal nightmare.

You're obviously competent. You're ambitious and dedicated. You like the people in the company. The problem, however, is that you really have a problem with your boss. It's not that she is abusive or dishonest, but her management style and her personality in general set your teeth on edge to the point that you hate being around her, and it's making you have second thoughts about whether you should be in that position at all.

Sound familiar? At times we find it difficult to understand why two civilized, mentally healthy people can drive each other crazy. But whether we call it bad chemistry, personality clashes, or not being on the same wavelength, some people are harder to get along with than others, and if one of those people is your manager, supervisor, or team leader, you can be in for a miserable time on the job.

BEFORE YOU TAKE THE JOB

Personal style differences in the workplace can wear on your nerves, particularly in already stressful and frantic work environments. If you find yourself working for a boss you just can't tolerate, no matter how much you like everything else about the company and your responsibilities, you'll probably still end up hating your job.

To avoid finding yourself in such a predicament, learn to spot potential personality issues during an interview, before you take the plunge. Knowing what to look for can help you avoid making a disastrous decision and make life easier once you're on the job. Of course, once you've decided to join a firm, efforts to establish a strong, mutually respectful working relationship with your manager will pay big dividends in your career development.

Know your own style and look for compatibility. When applying for any new position, make sure that you have a good idea about how you like to exchange information and interact with others. Do you warm up to people quickly or are you more reserved until you get to know someone? How's your sense of humor? Would you be happy working in an atmosphere that encourages good-natured bantering and even a few practical jokes, or do you embarrass easily or get your feelings hurt often? Do you prefer to work in an environment where collaboration and feedback are important, or would you rather work in solitude?

Think about what you would consider a perfect day at work. Is it an environment where you can accomplish your goals without interruptions, or does a successful day involve meetings with colleagues in group brainstorming sessions and talking to many different people?

You may be uncomfortable with a manager who gives you a few high-level instructions and sends you on your way with little guidance. Conversely, you may be frustrated by someone who checks on you too often, micromanaging even the simplest tasks. A clear understanding of your own style is an essential starting point for identifying the potential for conflict or compatibility with a manager.

Determine how your energy level will fit with your potential manager's. Will a supervisor who roars in every morning like a Category 5 hurricane stimulate or stymie your creativity? Do you appreciate a boss's calm, soothing style, or would you have an overwhelming urge to check his pulse? Recognize that people peak and slump at different times of day. Is the morning your best time to handle challenging assignments, or do you need to ease into your day? A manager who is most creative at 3:00 p.m. may be distressing to someone who was full of vigor at 10:00 in the morning but is hitting a low by mid-afternoon.

Although you probably don't want to work for your clone, it helps if you have a similar (or at least compatible) approach to work styles and interpersonal communication. That way, you won't waste your energy trying to avoid situations that irritate either of you and can concentrate on getting the job done.

Obviously, you can't completely assess someone's personality in an interview, but one's personal style can give you a good clue to what a person is like. Author and management consultant Pat MacMillan notes that observing personal style can give you some idea of what's underneath the surface—value systems, emotional maturity, and philosophies about dealing with people.

Pay attention to eye contact, voice inflection, and body language when meeting your prospective employer. Notice whether the handshake is firm or unenthusiastic. Observe the individual's general deportment. Does he or she come across as confident, arrogant, down-to-earth, or insecure? Does this person smile quickly, put you at ease immediately, and make conversation effortlessly, or is the person's behavior guarded and reserved?

In addition to demeanor, notice your interviewer's conversation style. Does he integrate the personal and the professional? Is he interested in whether your father is out of the hospital or that your daughter's soccer team won the city championship? Or does he appear to be all business, with little interest in what's going on outside the office?

Some managers view the world as a friendly place, full of basically good people with a few bad apples. Others see a world (customers, coworkers, the media, etc.) full of potential challenges that make them always ready to catch people goofing off or making mistakes. Look for clues about this person's managerial style. Do you hear a lot of "we" and "our," or is it primarily "I" and "mine"?

How people manage time and handle schedules can also affect the quality of your working life. Will you get plenty of warning about that huge presentation, or will you find out about it forty-eight hours before showtime? When you go to an interview, be aware of the surroundings. Check out the noise level and kinds of activities among current employees. Observe whether people seem stressed or relaxed. I've visited organizations where I can sense the tension the moment I walk into the office.

WHEN YOUR BOSS IS PROMOTED: HOW TO START OFF ON THE RIGHT FOOT WITH A NEW ONE . . .

➤ Take the initiative to make the new manager feel welcome.

➤ Position yourself as a source of pertinent information (not the department gossip).

➤ Ask your new boss to clarify his or her expectations and management style.

➤ If possible, speak to people who have worked for this manager.

➤ Discuss projects in which you are currently involved; at minimum, you'll want to get approval for continuing and let the new boss know the resources you'll need.

➤ Use the same techniques to discover your new manager's personality attributes as you used when interviewing for the job.

Ask questions to get a snapshot of your interviewer's personality. Come to the interview prepared to ask questions that will reveal information about your potential boss's personality, and notice the way your interviewer responds. Does she answer quickly or does she ponder issues before reacting? Does the fact that you're asking questions have an unsettling effect? Does she elaborate with examples and anecdotes, or do you get bare-bones facts and little else? When your prospective employer describes the job you are considering, pay attention to whether the interviewer focuses on goals and big-picture results or provides a lot of details about daily activities.

Just as a savvy interviewer will probably ask you behavior-based questions, you can do the same. You might, for example, inquire about how this person helps employees develop or how he deals with conflict. One way to find out more about a manager is to ask how he or she came to work for the company. People generally like to talk about major turning points in their lives, so listen carefully to what factors prompted the choice of workplace. It may reveal a good bit about what makes this person tick. Conversely, not getting much response to your questions may also tell you that this person may not be particularly forthcoming with information once you're on the job.

In some cases, you can gather some information by talking to current employees. For example, find out whether the manager makes most of the decisions and then informs everyone how it's going to be, or lets people do their thing—unless a crisis or something really important arises. If you prefer an autocratic style to one of more shared responsibility, you may feel at ease in such an environment. If, however, you like to be a part of the decision-making process and be accountable for results, both successes *and* failures, then you need to work for someone with a more participative approach.

ONCE YOU'RE ON BOARD

Making the success of your association a priority will benefit both you and your manager in the short and long term. At times, unfortunately, subtle personality differences surface after you have been working for a manager for a while. Even if things are going well, here are some suggestions on how to avoid any problems that might crop up in the future.

Maintain an open dialogue. As you interact with a manager, remember that solid working relationships don't develop overnight. Continue to let your boss know what encourages and motivates you while persisting in identifying what your manager needs from you. Always couch these conversations in terms of your desire to be a more effective contributor to the company and a valuable resource to your supervisor.

You may want a manager who can tolerate criticism and be willing to delegate. Or you may need a boss who is friendly and pleasant when things are going well and supportive when the chips are down. Do you require constant inspiration and sincere appreciation? Or do you spurn emotional appeals, believing that logic and objectivity are the mark of a mature individual?

One of the key components of a supervisor/employee relationship is feedback about performance. If you depend on frequent updates about what you are doing right and what you need to improve on, you'll be frustrated working for a manager who performs an annual performance review that focuses only on the problem areas. The "as long as you don't hear from me, things are okay" philosophy doesn't fly with those who look for positive reinforcement. On the other hand, if you're the type who wants a lot of freedom in which to do your job, micromanagement will frustrate both you and your manager. If possible, come to an agreement about the nature and frequency of feedback.

Use your manager's personality traits as an opportunity for self-examination. Your boss may criticize your tendency to be lenient on those members of your team who miss deadlines or skip assignments. Instead of writing off his criticism as a function of his dominating personality and need for control, consider whether you should learn to be more assertive. Being everyone's friend may make you popular with the troops, but you may not come across to those above you as senior management material because you appear unable to hold others accountable.

Ask for opportunities to get some training or work with a coach to help you develop an area in which you may be weak. Recognizing strengths in your manager doesn't mean that you should set out to imitate him or her to the extreme, but recognizing where your personality differences might stifle your opportunities for growth and promotion and looking for legitimate ways to narrow the gap will benefit both you and your manager.

Finally, you'll have an easier time if you recognize that your manager was simply born with a tendency toward a particular personality and isn't intentionally out to make your life miserable. If you have trouble dealing with your superior's personality, you essentially have two choices. If the situation becomes intolerable, you may want to seek another job, or you can acknowledge, accept, and learn to deal with your boss's personality and behavior. Ideally, you can become a beneficial ally, leveraging your strengths and differences to offset each other's quirks and ultimately to create a powerful team.

THE BOTTOM LINE

> ➤ Some people are harder to get along with than others, and if one of those people is your manager, supervisor, or team leader, you can be in for a miserable time on the job.

➤ Look for important verbal and nonverbal signals in the interview process.

➤ On the job, getting along with your manager requires open, ongoing communication and an ability to see both sides of the issue.

➤ Learning to deal with your manager's personality differences can help create a powerful work team.

CHAPTER 16

How to Speak So Your Boss Will Listen

*T*he workplace has changed. The old command-and-control manager is pretty much on the way out, replaced by fewer levels of management and a more collaborative atmosphere in most companies. Managers recognize the abilities of their employees, and organizations are more receptive than ever to the perspectives and solutions of their workforce.

Yet, many talented professionals struggle with how to communicate upward in the organization, without appearing to be presumptuous, self-serving, or manipulative. You may be forthright and assertive with coworkers or direct reports, but when it comes to communicating up the organization, you may doubt that you are doing the best job of selling your ideas, and yourself, to the higher-ups.

Most managers value employees who are able to master the art of upward communication, and those who have those skills are the ones who come to mind when opportunities arise. Communicating effectively with your manager requires that you combine assertiveness and respect, clarity and flexibility, the ability to articulate and the ability to listen.

Here are some guidelines for getting your boss's attention and achieving the rewards that result from developing this critical skill.

PLANNING AN APPROACH TO ACHIEVE RESULTS

Be prepared with your key points. Coming to your manager with a brainstorm that just popped into your head is a recipe for rejection. Curb your enthusiasm until you get the facts (both pro and con), find concrete examples to support your premise, and organize your message into a logical, well-developed presentation. As Eric Garner, author of "7 Rules of Upward Communication," notes, you may undermine your credibility if you have to go away and get more information.

If you are bringing a problem to your manager because you need his or her help, make sure that you have made every effort to resolve it yourself, and be prepared to report on what you have done so far.

And always, make efficient use of your manager's time. Your issues are only one of many the boss is addressing.

Put your message in the right perspective. Link your ideas to the goals and concerns of both your manager and the company at large. Before you meet with your manager, identify ways that your proposal can benefit others. Know what particular concerns are on your boss's mind—cutting costs, improving morale, or increasing sales. Focus your creativity in areas that will solve some of her problems.

Find out how other companies are handling similar situations, and have some solutions in mind. Managers like options and usually want to be part of the decision process. Even if you think you know the answer, don't stop there. Bring a couple of other possibilities and lay them all out for your manager to consider.

Be ready to answer questions. If you are proposing a new initiative or making your manager aware of a problem, make sure that you anticipate any questions he or she may ask. Pay attention to your manager's communication style. Does he look at things from a global perspective? Does she want to know your thought processes—how you arrived at your recommendation? Does your manager like details and count on you having the i's dotted and t's crossed, or expect your idea to be a work in progress? Have you spoken with anyone else or garnered advice from others in the company? Are you certain that your idea doesn't duplicate or conflict with other initiatives currently in process?

Don't interpret your manager's questions as a lack of trust in your judgment or a prelude to refusal. Avoid getting defensive and instead welcome the scrutiny. If you can answer the questions with poise and competence, you will solidify your chances for acceptance.

Speak with confidence. Deborah Tannen, in her *Harvard Business Review* article "The Power of Talk: Who Gets Heard and Why," reports that the CEO of a major corporation says that he will decide in five minutes about issues that someone may have been working on for five months. If the person proposing the initiative seems confident, the CEO usually approves it. If not, he rejects it. This approach may seem extreme, but it attests to the fact that you can't separate the message from the messenger. If you don't believe in your idea, why do you expect others to buy in?

Confidence comes from being thoroughly prepared and knowing that you have the ability to turn your concepts into reality. However, most of the executives I have interviewed warn that confidence shouldn't cross the line into arrogance. Always be willing to listen and to learn.

Obviously, every idea won't receive a big thumbs-up. If your manager says no, be gracious and appreciative of the fact that your boss listened to your request. Find out, without being defensive, why you didn't get the approval you desired and, if appropriate, ask what you should have done differently. Done correctly, the process will strengthen your long-term relationship with your manager and increase the chance of success for future proposals. Furthermore, your strengthened relationship will yield benefits in ways that you may not anticipate today.

Keep your manager in the loop. Once you get your manager's approval, don't disappear while you are working on the project. Bosses hate nasty surprises, such as finding out after the fact that you went over budget or over someone's head to get the job done. Give progress reports along the way, and make sure that you take your manager's advice to heart. The feedback that you incorporate may be the difference in success and failure. And you will get more buy-in about the finished product, too.

The ability to communicate effectively to those above you in an organization can be the talent that sets you apart. When you build a reputation for success in this area, you will give yourself and your message a decided advantage.

THE BOTTOM LINE

➤ Knowing how to communicate upward in the organization, without appearing to be presumptuous, self-serving, or manipulative, is a critical skill that is key to your success.

➤ Putting your message in the right perspective can make the difference between acceptance and rejection.

➤ Anticipating questions and being prepared to answer them with concrete data and examples will build your manager's confidence in your abilities.

➤ Keeping your manager apprised of your progress, after you receive approval, will avoid unpleasant surprises along the way.

CHAPTER 17

E-mail

Think Before You Send

*W*ithout question, e-mail is one of the great conveniences of modern society. By the same token, it can be intrusive and, in the extreme, overwhelming, threatening—flooding us with information and consuming our time to the point of being counterproductive because of its sheer volume and persistence. But however we feel about it, electronic mail is a fact of life in business and is a growing presence in our personal lives.

The Radicati Group, a technology marketing research firm, estimated that there were more than 4 billion e-mail accounts by the end of 2015. That translates to over 144 billion e-mails each day. Communicating by e-mail has become the status quo in our wired society, and for good reason. Its advantages are many. Perhaps most obvious is its speed and scope. With the click of a key, you can send a message from Boston to Beijing—unhampered by time zones and office hours and long-distance-calling charges. Far fewer rambling voice mails end up in our phone mailboxes, and telephone tag is no longer one of the leading nuisances at work. You can read or send messages at 3:00 a.m. on Saturday if you wish, and before you head out of the office for the day you can let *everyone* in the company know about the upcoming company picnic as easily as you tell a single person. We have become dependent on the amazing convenience.

Furthermore, e-mail has contributed to developing the flatter, more egalitarian organization, which most companies advocate. Employees typically feel more comfortable e-mailing someone in upper management than they would calling that person or knocking on a manager's door for a conversation. E-mail also makes it easier to share information, whether it's between team members, within a single department, or to every staff member in a global company. With e-mail, it's easier to keep people in the know and harder for people to claim that they "didn't get the word."

E-MAIL CAN BE TRICKY BUSINESS

With all its advantages, one might come to believe that e-mail is the greatest thing in organizational communication since the ballpoint pen. So why do so many people mention e-mail as one of the major communication problems in their workplace?

Because of the speed with which we can create one message and its lack of formality, e-mail can easily cause problems, misinform, waste time, and reflect poorly on the sender. Part of the problem lies in the fact that e-mail is a hybrid communication medium. It combines the spontaneity and informality of spoken communication with the permanence of written communication.

Conversely, with spoken communication, either in person or on the phone, the parties have a distinct advantage inherent in an interactive conversation. Tone of voice, inflection, and volume immediately invoke a response, and the interactive nature of the conversation promotes concurrence or a complete understanding by both parties. Obviously, when the parties are physically together, the most important attribute of spoken communication, body-language, contributes to fuller understanding of the message.

One of the advantages of written communication lies in the writer's ability to spend the necessary time crafting a message that says what he or she really intends to say—through drafting, editing, and proofreading. It enables the writer to translate thoughts into a clear, precise, and readable message that addresses all of the issues, contains the correct tone, and elicits the desired information or response from the recipient Many people seem to forget that e-mail is, in fact, written communication, and consequently they treat it much less carefully. Workplace e-mail messages often contain terse and offhand remarks and project a flippant attitude that is sometimes excessive, even bordering on the unprofessional. Some people who write the e-mails overlook how their message comes across to the receiver. When composing e-mails, many people don't seem to be nearly as concerned with structure and correctness as they would be when putting something on paper. This attitude is ironic because often many more people see an e-mail than would ever see a hard copy memo or letter because it's so easy for the recipient to forward an e-mail to anyone.

Here are some commonsense suggestions for ways to maximize the advantages of e-mail and avoid turning it into a self-inflicted disadvantage or worse, an obstacle to your success.

Know the recipient's communication preference. Some people still prefer other forms of communication over e-mail, often because the sheer number of e-mails (many of which are companywide or information-only messages) causes specific messages to get lost in the crowd.

I recently spoke on the telephone with a middle manager in a large utility company who remarked that he was, at that moment, looking at 139 unopened e-mails on his computer—and that was just for the current day. "I don't have any intention of going through them until much later," he said. "And I will delete most of them. If you really want to get a message to me, call me. I'll answer the phone if I'm there, and I always return my voice mails." Other people prefer texting or instant messaging. You will have a better chance of getting your message through if you know your receiver's communication preferences.

Consider the reader's disposition and perspective. Another tricky feature of written communication lies in the fact that the message is static once you send it. Unlike spoken messages, which you can quickly modify if you see the person getting annoyed or displeased, your written messages are vulnerable to the reader's mood, existing perceptions, and attitudes toward the subject—and toward you.

The more difficult or complex the message, the greater the opportunity for confusion, misinterpretation, or anger. If you find yourself struggling with the choice of words and the phrases as you write the e-mail, chances are you're dealing with a message that would work better in another form. Choose another medium, preferably face-to-face, but at the very least consider making a telephone call so that you can explain yourself and the other person can ask questions or clarify.

Know that an e-mail can produce unintended interpretations. Sometimes, perhaps because you sent the message off hurriedly or even because the receiver is not in the best of moods, an e-mail you send can be interpreted in a way that's entirely different from what you had in mind. In reply, the recipient may send a surly message or otherwise show his or her irritation.

Your first reaction may be to fire back a real zinger to justify or defend yourself. However, the wise choice may be to nip that exchange in the bud by changing the medium immediately. Pick up the telephone or, if possible, go to that person's office or cubicle and talk through the matter. Apologize for the misunderstanding, if necessary. The longer the tension festers, the bigger deal it will be. Catch it early, and both of you will forget it quickly.

Review before you send. Even if you don't consider the e-mail sensitive, review it a couple of times before you send it to make sure that your tone isn't brusque or demanding. Often something as simple as putting the word "please" in front of a sentence will soften the tone. If after reviewing the e-mail you're still uncertain about how the reader may receive it, put it in the "Draft" folder for a while. When you go back to it later, you can look at it with a fresh eye and judge it more objectively. If you're still not sure, consider having someone else look at it before you send it.

You should exercise the same care when you are replying to a message. Also, along with reviewing your message for the appropriate tone, make sure that your reply answers all the questions or addresses the issues the sender raised. Some time ago, I wrote an e-mail asking four specific questions to a woman at an organization where I was going to conduct a class on business writing. She responded with an answer to two of them. I sent her another e-mail, thanking her for her response but repeating the two unanswered questions. Her reply answered one of the two, with no reference to the other question. I had to call to get an answer to the final question.

Remember that less formality doesn't mean anything goes. E-mail's informality and conversational style can make the message readable and personal, but don't confuse informality with carelessness. As in any written communication, the errors can stay around to haunt you for a long time. While most people are more tolerant of the occasional typo in e-mail messages, they will notice consistent violations of spelling, grammar, and structure, and their opinion of you will doubtless be influenced by it. Use standard punctuation and capitalization, and edit your e-mails carefully for grammar, punctuation, and spelling. (Don't forget to use the spell check feature, but don't rely on it completely.) Remember that punctuation misuse can change the meaning of your sentence altogether. Note how punctuation changes the meanings of the following sentences:

> *A woman without her man is nothing.*
> *A woman: without her, man is nothing.*

You get the idea.

Also keep in mind that using all caps in your e-mails is a no-no. I hear frequent complaints about e-mails written in all caps. Use of all caps gives the impression that the sender is shouting. However, a more practical reason for not using all capital letters is that they are harder to read. Reading involves visually collecting the symbols on the page and telegraphing them to the brain. Since all caps are similar in height and width, sorting the information and getting it to its destination takes longer. In fact, all caps can slow reading time by as much as 15 percent.

Similarly, writing in all lower case is not desirable either, since we are accustomed to seeing sentences and proper nouns start with capital letters.

Use sarcasm, humor, or jargon sparingly—if at all. Being conversational also includes the temptation to use humor, sarcasm, or industry jargon, sometimes excessively. Remember that in written communication, you depend entirely on the words; you don't have the support from your voice and body language to reinforce that you were only kidding when you made that stinging remark. All the receiver of the message has to work with is your words and his or her interpretation. For that reason, writing in a straightforward manner is a smart move.

Even if you follow your biting or sarcastic remarks with an emoticon—those little icons that signify emotions, such as the colon followed by the right parenthesis to indicate a smiley face—you may still come across as condescending or insincere. Limit or avoid any remarks that your reader may misinterpret—particularly if you don't know that person well.

Use the same courtesy that you would in a face-to-face conversation or a formal letter. "Please," "Thank you," "I hope you're well," and "Have a nice weekend" are little touches that don't take much time but put a thoughtful, human face on your message. Think of what you would be saying to that person if you were having a "live" conversation, and use the same courtesies that you would in that situation. Although taking the time to be courteous may sound trivial, or even condescending, many normally polite people seem to forget their manners when sending e-mails.

And while we're on the subject of courtesy, use courtesy titles if you are e-mailing someone for the first time. If "Mr. Gray" wants you to call him "Tom," he can let you know that by signing his reply with just his first name. Even if you feel comfortable using someone's first name, avoid assuming that the person responds to a nickname. Charles may not want to be "Chuck," David may hate "Dave," and Gwendolyn may not like "Gwen." People's names are extremely important to them; don't take liberties with them.

Don't circulate e-mails with offensive or defamatory content. If you receive such e-mails, delete them immediately and politely ask the sender not to send any more e-mails to you. Having those e-mails in your inbox could cause problems for both you and your organization, particularly if you work for a large company.

Compose a clear subject line. If your e-mails are going to penetrate the gridlock of blast messages, general information, spam, and trivia, you need to take steps to get the reader's attention. One way is to start with an attention-getting subject line. This "heads up" can let the recipient know what he or she can expect from the text that follows. Rather than a subject line such as "Our conversation" try "Answers to your question about next year's training budget." By jogging the reader's memory and making the e-mail relevant, you improve your chances of getting a quick response if you need one. In addition, you make it easier for the recipient to identify the contents of the e-mail in the future, should the person be searching for specific information. And, if the focus changes during the e-mail exchange, make sure that you update your subject line.

Use the "Urgent" or "Important" designation with care. If you overdo it, you won't get the reader's attention when something is really urgent or important.

Opinions vary about whether to keep the thread of all the messages within a series of e-mails. You do that, of course, by hitting "Reply" rather than "New Message" to respond to the sender. Some people suggest that the person who sent the original message doesn't need to see it again, but after a topic has gone back and forth a few times, over hours or even days, it's often helpful to get the whole picture in one e-mail rather than having to go back to the inbox to reconstruct the history.

Keep your e-mail messages short—no more than a full screen. A long message will fall into the "I'll read it later" category, which often translates to "never." If you need to communicate a long message, send it in hard copy or attach it to the e-mail as a separate document. However, in the latter case, first make sure that your recipient has the software to open your attachment.

Respect each other's privacy. Privacy is in short supply in a world of easily accessible information. Using electronic mail exposes you and your recipients to contacts they may not want. If you're mailing to a list, use mail merge or send the e-mail to yourself, with the mailing list as a blind carbon copy (bcc). That way none of the recipients will see each other's e-mail addresses. Also out of respect for other's privacy, always ask permission before forwarding another person's e-mail. And never edit or change the original message. Sarah Myers McGinty, author of *Power Talk: Using Language to Build Authority and Influence,* suggests either summarizing the original e-mail or cutting and pasting a small section. When you're the original sender of a message, and you don't mind having the receiver forward it, indicate your permission at the beginning of the message.

Reply in a timely manner. One of the main attributes of e-mail is its immediacy. People send e-mails because they generally expect a quick response. Respond to your e-mails, preferably within the same business day but certainly within twenty-four hours. If you can't deal with the e-mail's content within that time, reply to the sender acknowledging that you received the message and stating when you will respond.

Use the "Reply to All" feature with care. Unless everyone who got the original e-mail really needs to see your reply, simply reply to the person who sent the e-mail. This practice helps avoid needless clutter in everyone else's inbox and the waste of time reading irrelevant messages.

Never reply to spam. Avoid becoming an appealing target to spammers by never responding to spam. Even when you send the "Remove me from the list" message, by opening and replying to spam you are confirming that you have a working e-mail address, exactly what the spammers want to know. Simply delete spam or use a program that filters it automatically.

LEVERAGING EMAIL'S ADVANTAGES

Even though we all sometimes complain about how many e-mails we receive, e-mail offers a great opportunity to stay in touch with very little effort. If you are alert to its pitfalls and take the necessary steps to avoid careless wording or thoughtless comments, as well as unnecessarily flooding others with information they don't need, you can use this tool to increase your visibility and impress others with your efficiency, expertise, and ability to share information. Handled effectively, e-mail remains today's major way to remain current and in the communication loop.

THE BOTTOM LINE

- ➤ Communicating by e-mail has become the status quo.
- ➤ E-mail has contributed to creating more egalitarian organizations.
- ➤ Even with its advantages, e-mail is not a total communication solution.
- ➤ Following certain guidelines will help you maximize the advantages and avoid the missteps of using e-mail in today's business environment.

CHAPTER 18

Using Your Phone Most Productively

*B*efore the Internet, with its stunning power and flexibility, changed the way we work, the telephone was our fastest and most efficient method for overcoming both great distances and busy schedules.

Easy to use, reliable, and relatively inexpensive, it became the most pervasive communication tool in business—both an enabler and an intruder. It changed people's lives in many ways, not unlike the explosion of all-encompassing broadband and wireless access has today. And even though e-mail has taken its place in many cases, the telephone still frequently is the communication tool of choice. One reason is that the telephone is often a convenient alternative to conversing face-to-face and because it provides a richer communication opportunity than written words.

TELEPHONE BASICS

For all its advantages, telephone communication certainly has its pitfalls, but handling this communication medium efficiently and courteously can pay big dividends in terms of your productivity and success. Here are some simple, but sometimes overlooked, rules to keep in mind.

Recognize the importance of your voice. In telephone conversation, the immediacy of spoken communication is retained, but the important visual cues inherent in a face-to-face conversation—posture, eye contact, facial expression, or gestures—are lost. For that reason, when communicating by phone, your voice becomes much more important in the interaction because it must carry some of the load usually handled by your body language. You need to rely on the three P's—Pitch, Pace, and Power—to create the variety and energy necessary to command and keep your audience's attention. You can achieve this objective by sitting up straight in your chair, breathing deeply for sufficient vocal power, gesturing as you would in a normal conversation, and keeping your eyes off your computer screen if you happen to be near it. Some communication coaches even recommend standing when talking on the phone because this allows the speaker to naturally convey more energy.

When You Are the Caller

Plan your agenda before you call. If necessary, make some notes before you place the call, identifying the two or three points you want to address while you have that person on the line. If you fail to establish your agenda, the other party—who may have his or her own agenda—may have the upper hand in the conversation.

Organize your conversation so that the other person can follow and remember. Use transitions and connector words just as you would in writing a memo. "Hello, Luis. It's Taylor. I need to let you know about two issues. First, remember that Miriam is leaving on maternity leave on the twenty-first of this month, and we still need to decide on how we're going to fill that slot. And next, I just heard from Kim Imports and it can't ship until Monday."

Place your own phone calls. If you have time to make a telephone call, you have time to place it. Having an assistant call for you and then put the receiver on hold while you come to the phone is inexcusable in most situations. Doing so sends a huge message to the person you called that your time is much more important that anyone else's.

Get the go-ahead before you begin a lengthy conversation. Remember that unless you have a scheduled appointment to speak with someone on the telephone, you are intruding into that person's day. When you get Mr. Washington on the phone, immediately ask if he is available for a short conversation, or let him know that you intend to make it quick. Acknowledging that you recognize the importance of the person's time shows respect and concern for his situation.

Identify yourself quickly and clearly. Even if your recipient has Caller ID (which doesn't always work if you go through a company switchboard) or if you talk to the person frequently, identify yourself immediately. If this person has an assistant, identify yourself and, if appropriate, say why you're calling. For example: "Hello, Helen. This is Ross Ortiz. I'm returning Ms. Chapman's call."

If you have to call someone at home and the spouse or partner answers, let that person know who you are and ask if the person is available to take your call. If appropriate, apologize for calling the person at home and provide a general reason for your call. "Mrs. Owen, Mr. Owen wanted to have the quarterly sales numbers to prepare for tomorrow's meeting."

Use the speakerphone judiciously and courteously. Speakerphones are a great assistance when the call involves more than one person on one end or if you need your hands to perform some function, such as taking notes on a computer. However, you should never use the speaker feature without first asking the person you have called if he or she is agreeable to conducting a phone call that is less than private. Although most people can tell if they are engaging in a call in which the other person is using the speaker, you should still acknowledge that you are choosing this option. Furthermore, if anyone else is in the room, you have an ethical obligation to tell the person to whom you are talking that another person will hear what is being said. The other people in your office should also greet the person you have called and identify themselves.

Consider teleconferencing. In a teleconference, you may or may not use the speaker function, but generally more than two people participate in the conversation, often by accessing a teleconferencing service. A teleconference may be a good alternative to a meeting if the conversation is primarily informational in nature, but it doesn't work well for handling sensitive issues or for conducting negotiations. The delays inherent in the technology limit one's ability to speak quickly (or almost simultaneously), while the formality of the process makes spontaneous conversation impossible. Therefore, if you predict a heated discussion, you might want to reconsider using this format. If you actually want the callers to participate, limit the number of participants so that everyone has time to speak during the allotted time.

If you are leading a teleconference, make sure that you introduce everyone on the line and indicate their location and their interest in the discussion. At the end of the call, summarize the conversation and reiterate any action items before ending the session. Thank everyone for participating in the discussion. Following up with an e-mail that summarizes the conference is also a good idea.

As a teleconference participant, these guidelines can make the call go more smoothly:

- ➤ Identify yourself each time you speak, particularly if the group is large and if you don't regularly meet by telephone with these people.
- ➤ Organize your comments for clarity.
- ➤ Pay attention and avoid offline chats.
- ➤ Avoid interrupting or responding curtly.
- ➤ If you have to leave the call, let people know that you are disengaging.

Treat a voice mail message like a memo. If you can't reach the party you are calling and choose to leave voice mail, make sure your message is efficient and meaningful. Since a great number of telephone calls originate for the sole purpose of exchanging information, you may be able to take care of business as effectively as if the person were actually there to answer the phone.

If you do need someone to call you back, you can save everyone time if you give the person a preview of why you called. A voice mail that says, "Joe, it's Marie. Call me" doesn't give him a chance to prepare for the return call. Think of the memo format with its "To," "From," "Date," and "Subject" lines. Since most voice mail systems are date-and time-stamped, you may not need to say when you called. So your message can go something like this: Joe, this is Marie Marsh. I checked on the availability of the conference room that you suggested for the fifteenth, and unfortunately it's booked. A similar room on the fifth floor is available. Let me know, either by returning this call or by e-mail, if that room will work. I'll be here until six today."

If you can't deliver a message in a half-dozen sentences or so, let the person know that you need to discuss the matter at more length. No one wants to listen to interminable voice mails, and if you have a habit of leaving them, people will start to hit the erase button without listening to the entire message.

Check before you speak. Occasionally, instead of reaching the person you're calling, you will reach an assistant or someone else in the office, whose function it is to screen calls and sometimes keep calls from reaching their destination.

If you don't mind stating the purpose of your call, state it when you first ask to speak to the individual you're calling. Your forthcoming nature may make the gatekeeper feel more comfortable putting you through. If you are returning a person's call, or if someone suggested that you call that person, by all means say so. If you suspect, however, that stating your purpose will not facilitate a connection, say politely that you have a matter that you really need to discuss with the individual you are asking for. You might add, "I've checked and clearly Ms. Rivera is the person to whom I should speak in this case."

When You Receive a Call

Answering a call requires much of the same behavior as placing one, except this time you aren't in the driver's seat. Although you certainly can decide when to take your calls at work, avoid hiding behind voice mail to keep from talking to people. Remember that a huge part of communication is building relationships. You never know when a productive or friendly telephone conversation may make a favorable impression on a customer, client, or coworker that will pay dividends in the future.

Speak clearly and perhaps a bit more slowly than usual. Mechanical reproduction of your voice isn't the same as hearing you live, and we discern what our ears miss with our eyes in a face-to-face conversation. State your name clearly, and speak slowly so that someone whose first language may not be the same as yours can pick up the nuances of pronunciation.

Provide pertinent information, but avoid a monologue. Callers usually know what company and department they have called by the time they get to the person answering a call. For example, "Piedmont Central University, College of Business, Management Department,

Jane Hill, how may I help you?" is a little much. If you need to state your department or title along with your name, make your voice sound helpful and leave off the added baggage. "Management Department, Jane Hill speaking," gets the call on its way. If you are answering the call for someone else, identify that person and yourself as well. "Mary Grant's office, this is Clarice."

Be considerate when you receive a call. If you need to put the caller on hold to gather some information, ask that person's permission, estimate the length of the hold time, and offer to call the person back. "Please hold"—click—makes people feel like a door just got slammed in their faces.

If someone catches you at a bad time, or when you need to keep the line open for an urgent call, let the caller know in a respectful way that you are not available at the moment (in most cases you can use voice mail to catch calls you don't want to answer) and say when you'll call back. Make sure that you honor your commitment.

If you do take the call, focus your attention on the caller and the message. Turn away from your computer screen and summon your listening skills. Listen for both the words and the "music"—any signals that you may be able to pick up from the voice or the emotions of the speaker. If you're not sure about something, ask for clarification.

Keep the conversation businesslike. Avoid chitchat unless the receiver of your call seems receptive. One of the great advantages of e-mail is that the recipient can choose when and where to access that message. Phone calls don't offer the same flexibility. For that reason, you should be particularly mindful of your receiver's time. Keep the discussion on track and your answers to the point. Getting to the point, however, doesn't mean being abrupt or insensitive. If the caller seems to want to engage in small talk, accommodate if you have the time. If you are the one who is rushed, apologize for being in a hurry and mention that you would like to catch up when both of you have more time.

If you are returning someone's call, but you also have some information or want to address an additional issue, allow the person you're calling to tell you the reason for the original call before launching into your own message.

MAKE THE MEDIUM WORK FOR YOU AND OTHERS

Being effective on the telephone can give you a competitive edge in many situations because so many of us use it poorly. Every so often, ask close associates how you present yourself on the telephone and if they would suggest any adjustments to your phone style and manners. If you're really serious, try recording yourself occasionally to hear what your receiver hears.

The telephone is still a great tool for getting our messages across. Although we have more alternatives today, the telephone can reap significant rewards, if you leverage its advantages.

THE BOTTOM LINE

- ➤ The telephone is often a simple alternative to conversing face-to-face.
- ➤ When using the telephone, you keep the immediacy of spoken communication but lose the important visual cues inherent in face-to-face conversation.
- ➤ Your voice becomes much more important in the interaction since it must carry some of the load usually handled by your body language.
- ➤ Plan your message and get to the point quickly.
- ➤ Use speakerphones and teleconferencing judiciously.
- ➤ Mind your manners when you are answering a call.

CHAPTER 19

Dress Code Confusion

A client visiting your office hesitates to get on the elevator with a couple of scruffy-looking characters. Is she in the wrong place? Are these loiterers hanging out in your building up to no good? It turns out that these are two of your fellow employees on the way back to the office from lunch. It just happens to be dress-down Friday, and they've taken the casual initiative to a whole new level.

The ever-relaxing guidelines about dress, both for business and pleasure, may be sending mixed messages about who we are and how we feel about the situations in which we live, work, and socialize. We see jeans along with a tuxedo jacket at a "black tie optional" event. We receive an engraved invitation to a cocktail party and arrive to find many of the guests dressed as though they just returned from a trip to the grocery store. Does this lack of formality herald a more relaxed society or a general lack of respect for (or lack of understanding of) general conventions of appropriateness and good taste? What does our overly casual appearance say to the executive who has carved out time to hear our presentation or to the client who has opened his or her home to us?

Casual days started in the 1980s both as a response to a less formal working environment and as a way to reward employees in an era of downsizing and flattening of organizations. Permitting people to "dress down" seemed to be a win-win situation. In many companies, employees eagerly looked forward to Fridays (the most popular day for going casual), and many studies showed that, at first, productivity and morale both benefited from the initiative.

What started as a break from the daily routine, however, has become the norm in many companies. Indeed, most employees now consider wearing whatever they wish to work to be an entitlement rather than a perk. Additionally, going casual at work, where people once dressed for success, has had an effect outside the workplace, giving momentum to an increased disregard for protocol and tradition.

THE PACKAGING MATTERS

Although in many ways the trend toward less pretentious and expensive wardrobes is refreshing and healthy, before you go too far, think about what you may be giving up. Unlike members of the animal kingdom, we don't sport feathers and fur to denote our status, position, or intentions. Instead, it's the clothing we wear that alerts people to how they should perceive us, and even how we perceive ourselves. But we often forget that, just as plumage sends a message, clothing speaks volumes about us.

Indeed, clothing is part of the package that affects people's impression of us, particularly when they meet us for the first time, and whether we like it or not, most of that first impression comes from the visual impact that we make.

When you present yourself, especially in a business situation, much of your success may depend on the credibility that you project and the resulting confidence that you inspire in those you need to impress. You know by now that credibility comes from more than just being good at what you do or even having a good command of language. It comes from the overall package you present, a package that includes what you're wearing. According to *Forbes* contributor David Williams, "The visual aesthetic we present to others through our appearance and apparel is extremely important." The less credibility you have from other sources (let's say you are starting out in your career, for example, and don't have a track record), the more you may have to rely on your external presence to make that first impression. As time goes by, of course, other factors coalesce to define your capabilities. For example, if you've led your team or division to consistent success and double-digit earnings for ten years running, you can wear just about anything you want and still convey the necessary authority. In this case, your ultracasual attire may earn you the label of "eccentric" or "creative" instead of "slouch."

Although dress codes in the workplace will continue to change, there are a few simple guidelines you can follow to strike the right balance.

DO'S AND DON'TS OF BUSINESS CASUAL

Business Casual Is . . .

➤ Tailored jackets

➤ Tailored, well-fitting slacks

➤ Silk, cotton, or microfiber tees or blouses

➤ Basic colors, solids, stripes, checks (floral prints less acceptable)

➤ Skirts that are on the conservative side and generally accepted length in business situations (avoiding extremes either short or long and flowing)

➤ Golf shirts

➤ Khakis (pants or skirts)

➤ Pants suits for women

➤ Closed-toe shoes

Business Casual Isn't . . .

➤ See-through clothing

➤ Flip-flops

➤ Strappy sandals, particularly with high heels

➤ Shorts or cut-off jeans or jeans with holes

➤ Thigh-high boots with miniskirts

➤ Halter or tank tops

➤ Sweats

➤ T-shirts with logos or potentially offensive statements

➤ Scrunchies or banana clips for hair

Err on the side of moderation. Even if your organization operates in a business casual atmosphere, remember that business casual (as nebulous as that term may be) usually does not include nose rings, torn jeans, super miniskirts, or pants that show your underwear. Many businesses also consider sandals or flip-flops, T-shirts with clever (or obscene) phrases on them, and exercise gear unacceptable workplace attire. On the other hand, in most cases, business casual does include button-down collar shirts (no tie), well-cut pants suits for women, khakis or wool pants or skirts with jackets, and polo-type shirts with slacks. Keep in mind that when choosing casual wear, the cut, fit, and quality are particularly important because casual clothes are likely to be unlined or lightly structured. For this reason, consider investing in a higher quality casual wardrobe, particularly if the outfits are going to pull double-duty for work and play. Also, while it's a good idea to stay in sync with the rest of the staff—assuming most people dress appropriately and you don't want to put too much distance between yourself and your coworkers—lean toward the dressy side of casual. This practice may work in your favor because you'll stand out just enough to create an image of professionalism and success. It's a good idea, too, to stash a tie, a jacket, a pair of dress shoes, or whatever "emergency kit" items are appropriate in your office in case there's an unplanned visit to or from a client or customer.

It pays to keep in mind that, casual or not, it's still business, and what you wear can affect your career. Not long ago, a talented young woman in a consulting firm missed out on an opportunity to meet with senior executives of a client company because she had chosen that day to come to work more dressed down than was appropriate to her firm. She was unhappy that the CEO of her firm refused to take her with him on the call, but the client company was one in which the dress code was more traditional and even a bit formal.

Recognize that the same rules apply to out-of-office business functions. When you're attending a work-related social function (or any social function for that matter), try to determine the dress code preference of your host/hostess, and respect that person's turf. In social situations, what you wear speaks volumes about how you feel about the event. For example, if you show up at a black tie event in khakis and a blazer, or arrive at a wedding in a golf shirt, you are making a negative statement about the occasion's validity or significance. Furthermore, if you are at a function where you will be surrounded by colleagues and clients, your image in that social setting must be consistent with the polished and professional image you strive to project at work. Even if the invitation says casual (or even "elegantly casual"), get some clarification if you have any doubts about what is expected.

Knowing that you are dressed appropriately will give you added confidence, particularly in unfamiliar surroundings. People around you will also feel more comfortable.

Understand that the way you dress often affects the way you behave. Catch a glimpse of yourself in a mirror or a plate glass window occasionally. Note your stance, gait, and posture when you're dressed down in jeans and a T-shirt or slacks and a sweater. Then notice yourself when you are wearing either business or formal attire—when you are turned out to perfection. Chances are that you project more confidence when you're dressed more formally, because your demeanor often takes its cue from what you're wearing.

This correlation between clothes and behavior means that extremely casual dress codes may work well in a highly motivated, energized environment where everyone is totally committed to achieving a specific goal, but such environments are usually transitory—and difficult to maintain once the situation changes. When the shift inevitably occurs, too much casual can contribute to a playful, vacation atmosphere, which taken to excess may appear unprofessional and may actually have a negative effect on productivity. Therefore, even when the work culture permits it, don't wear your couch-potato weekend clothes to work, and if you're in a leadership role, discourage others from doing so. You know that your closet contains A-list casual attire and even some D-list items. All casual attire isn't equal. Use good judgment when you choose your clothing for the day.

Don't confuse casual dress with casual grooming. No matter how relaxed the dress code, be rigorous about how well you put yourself together. Make sure that you take care of all the details of hygiene and good grooming, with proper attention to hair, makeup, and nails. And before you leave the house, take a 360-degree look at yourself to make sure that you look good from all angles.

Remember that it's ultimately your call. Although it's unlikely that we'll return to the regimented business "uniforms" of times past, we still would do well to remember that appearance continues to give us the competitive edge that may make the critical difference in a given situation. In choosing your attire carefully with your objectives in mind, you have a great tool to help you send just the right message about yourself—depending on the situation and the audience. And, in a more practical vein, remember also that well-tailored business attire can disguise or minimize a multitude of figure flaws, something a tight-fitting knit shirt just can't do for you.

THE BOTTOM LINE

➤ Your credibility comes, at least in part, from the first impression you make.

➤ When in doubt, choose moderation.

➤ The way you dress affects the way you behave.

➤ Be aware of dress codes for business functions away from the office.

➤ Casual dress doesn't mean casual grooming.

CHAPTER 20

Mastering the Art of Meetings

*S*omeone once said that a successful meeting consists of three people: one who is out sick and another who is out of town. We all have experienced meetings that get off track because of the participants (some of whom shouldn't even be there), or because they last too long and accomplish too little. We sit there boiling with frustration, thinking about all the work that we could be doing if we weren't stuck in a nonproductive gathering where people show up unprepared, rehash old news, state the obvious, and leave with little intention of following up or following through on the decisions that emerged from the chaos.

The sad truth is that we know better. Meeting specialists and management consultants have been giving great advice for a quarter century, providing us with some sure-fire ways to make our meetings productive, yet we either forget them or hesitate to use them because either we lack the discipline or we are part of a corporate culture that has let bad meeting habits hang around for years.

Even if you can't change everything about meetings in your world, considering and implementing these four tips on meeting efficiency can help you make substantial progress toward eliminating meetings that undermine morale and stifle productivity.

MEETING EFFICIENCY TIPS

Be Sure you need to have a meeting. Meetings are critical to doing business successfully. Leveraging the power of the collective IQ can produce results that exceed what we can do alone. Effective meetings are great ways to inspire, ignite, and initiate solutions to problems and to build strong working relationships. In productive meetings, people feel heard and valued, and you can generate greater buy-in regarding decisions and changes in the organization.

In many cases, however, you can use other tools to share much of the information that has traditionally taken place in meetings. You don't always have to get people physically together in a room or on a conference call to get things done. For example, you can handle the FYI items, which clog far too many meetings, with e-mails or postings on a website.

Think of meetings as phantom investments. If you translate the salaries of the people who attend a typical meeting in your organization to an hourly rate, you will be amazed at how much that meeting actually costs. Companies that would never squander the company's tangible resources don't seem to mind wasting big dollars in meetings that you could have handled in other ways.

Deliver the agenda ahead of time. In addition to a start and end time, your agenda should have the date, location, and purpose of the meeting. Let others know who else will be attending, and articulate the nature of the meeting. Is it an information-gathering, problem-solving, or decision-making meeting? Do you want input, or are you delivering information? Do you need people to do anything before they arrive? What do you expect to occur as a result of that meeting?

Set the tone. Open the meeting with a short statement about the problems, objectives, and procedures of the meeting. Note the boundaries and constraints of your discussion. What will you discuss? What will the meeting not address? What methods or formats will you use to achieve your purpose? Keep your opening remarks under five minutes. If you speak too long, you will establish yourself as the meeting dominator rather than the meeting facilitator.

Assign a gatekeeper. If you are leading the meeting, a gatekeeper can keep the discussion on track and help manage the time you spend on each agenda item. Choose a gatekeeper who the group respects and likes and who will be firm but not heavy-handed. This person should make sure that the discussion stays true to the agenda, and also clarify assignments going forward. Lack of follow-up and follow-through are some of the most common complaints regarding unproductive meetings. You might also have your gatekeeper be your follow-up person to ensure that participants are indeed completing their post-meeting assignments, unless you assign a note taker to that duty.

Set ground rules. Think about the behaviors in meetings that detract from productivity (e.g., late arrivals, side conversations, digressions, lack of participation). Then consider the behaviors you want to instill in your meetings, such as active participation, focus on the task, and respect for others' ideas. Using the four or five attributes that you consider important, create some active ground rules that everyone can accept and follow. If everyone recognizes the ground rules (which you should post in the meeting room), your gatekeeper should have an easier time telling a vice president that it's not her turn to talk.

With increased emphasis on teams and matrix management, this ability to work productively in groups has assumed critical importance. Today, your reputation may depend more than your realize on your ability to lead and participate in the many kinds of meetings that organizations conduct. Once you establish yourself as an effective meeting leader, participants will look forward to contributing to the solutions and productivity that your meetings enable.

THE BOTTOM LINE

> ➤ Meetings are phantom investments that can be costly to companies if they are ineffective.
> ➤ Proper planning can increase the meeting's chance of success.
> ➤ Clear roles and responsibilities are critical to making a meeting run smoothly.
> ➤ Ground rules create agreed-upon behaviors that anticipate and address meeting derailers.

CHAPTER 21

When Meetings Go Virtual

*N*ew technology offers a low-cost alternative to face-to-face meetings. From check-ins with clients to regular staff meetings among different units of a company, "virtual" meetings help avoid the costs and wasted time of business travel. Of course, face-to-face meetings will never disappear: You will rarely make a real connection to colleagues or customers through electronic devices, no matter how sophisticated. While you may simulate walking into the meeting room and sitting down at the conference table in the virtual meetings offered by GoToMeeting.com, for example, your avatar won't replicate your body language, the tone of your voice, or even the concern on your face.

In short, virtual meetings can replace face-to-face meetings if the conversation is primarily informational in nature. However, like teleconferencing, they don't work well for handling contentious or sensitive issues or for conducting negotiations. If you expect a heated discussion, you should consider a different format. If you actually want the attendees to participate, limit the number of participants so that everyone has time to speak during the allotted time.

LEADING THE VIRTUAL MEETING

If you are leading a virtual meeting, the following steps will help ensure a productive event.

Invest in and learn to use video effectively. Jaleh Bisharat, Senior Vice President of Marketing, Elance-oDesk, notes that you will almost always benefit from being able to see your colleagues. Sharing slides or documents and hearing everyone speak may work well in a short meeting, but investing in the technology to allow videoconferencing will pay big dividends in the long run.

When scheduling, keep in mind time zone differences. While it is not always possible when uniting participants from different continents, try to avoid local lunch hours and extremely early or late meeting times.

Send materials out early. Ensure that participants receive the agenda and any meeting materials in plenty of time to prepare for the meeting.

Rehearse the technology. Give yourself ample time before the meeting to fix any technological problems that might arise. For example, rehearse using your audiovisual materials. If your office offers the resource, alert an AV person to the fact that you are having a meeting and the time the meeting will take place. Get this tech's direct contact information and, if possible, have the person on call.

Create a private environment. On the day of the meeting, make sure that you are in a room with closed doors so that no one will interrupt you and your colleagues won't hear a lot of extraneous noise. Put a sign on the door that a virtual meeting is in progress.

Introduce the participants. Start the meeting by introducing every participant and indicating their location and their interest in the discussion. If this is a mass meeting, you might introduce the groups involved (e.g., "From the UK, we have our London-based marketing team attending.")

Encourage remote attendees to speak first, or have a format for eliciting their comments. As in any meeting, if you begin by dominating the conversation, the participants, particularly those who aren't present, will tend to check out or feel uncomfortable about trying to break into the conversation. In your role as the meeting's leader, call on some of them directly. If the meeting is small enough, create some questions that demand a response from everyone.

Leave time for Q & As. Allow participants to ask questions, although at some point you will have to end the opportunity for Q & A. Some virtual meeting programs allow a chat function that will let people submit their questions in text. Provide an e-mail address to which participants can send further questions that come to mind.

Summarize the takeaways. At the end of the meeting, summarize the conversation and reiterate any action items before ending the session. Thank everyone for participating in the discussion. Following up with an e-mail that summarizes the meeting is also a good idea. If you don't have the time, delegate someone to follow up on the action item with the appropriate person.

AVOIDING VIRTUAL RUDENESS

Many of the same rules for face-to-face meetings, such as not interrupting or dominating the conversation, apply to virtual meetings—although virtual meetings can sometimes be more forgiving: The mute button allows you to unwrap that granola bar silently, and the fragrances of your Italian sub aren't shared with all participants. However, the distance in virtual meetings between you and the other participants may not be as great as you believe (e.g., everyone can hear when someone opens and closes the door behind you.) Therefore, here are some important courtesy rules for participants to follow when attending virtual meetings.

Make sure that you have received and looked at all materials. During the meeting is not the time to realize that you cannot follow the discussion because you weren't aware of the two articles to read beforehand. And the last thing you want to do is interrupt the meeting to ask the facilitator to resend the articles.

If the virtual meeting is a videoconference, dress in basic colors, but not black or white. Remember that you will be on a screen; bright colors and exuberant prints, as well as large, shiny jewelry, will be distracting.

Be on time. Don't believe that because the meeting is virtual you will be able to surreptitiously join the meeting without causing any disruption. Depending on the system you use, bells, beeps, or automated voices may notify everyone that Joel just joined the meeting. Or a pop-up window may let everyone know that you're late. In addition, the meeting facilitator will usually want to acknowledge a new presence. If possible, virtual meetings may be even more difficult to sneak into than a large live one.

Pick a quiet room. Although you are a participant, you should avoid any open-plan areas; the conversations of your colleagues will be distracting when meeting participants are trying to listen to what you have to say.

Identify yourself each time you speak. This practice is useful particularly if the group is large and if you don't regularly meet with these people.

Organize your comments for clarity. Even with visual capabilities, you must be able to connect with others through your voice. Others will easily disengage if you ramble, can't get to the point quickly, or fill your sentences with muttered "uhs," "wells," and "you knows." Know what you are going to say, and speak clearly and slowly to overcome the inevitable dip in sound quality that comes from speaking through machines. Make sure that you maintain appropriate vocal volume throughout your sentences. Avoid letting your voice trail off as you get to the end of your statement.

Pay attention and avoid off-line chats. You're wasting your time and the company's money if you are not really attending the meeting you are supposed to be attending. Turn off instant updates of e-mails—they will be too difficult to ignore. And don't believe that virtual meetings will allow you to get ready for your part of a meeting in the meeting. You should be prepared to participate fully before the meeting starts.

Catch the pauses to contribute. As with any meeting, at some point you will want to interject a comment without rudely interrupting. Wait until there's an appropriate break in the conversation or in the presentation from the meeting facilitator and then make your point clearly and succinctly. The art in contributing to any meeting is in catching the pause, almost like a surfer catching a wave. The slight delays inherent in long-distance communication can make the process more difficult, though, and unlike when you're engaged in a live conversation, you aren't able to detect all of the subtle changes in people's body language when they want to say something.

Use your mute capability generously. Noise is amplified. If you are going to cough or shuffle sheets of papers as you look for the latest sales figures, hit that button. Just remember to take it off when you're finished or you will wonder why people are speaking over your comments.

Keep body movement minimal. On the screen, any big body movement will be distracting to other participants. Although in a live encounter, gestures help support your message, when you are on-screen, "happy hands" can be a huge distraction.

Don't disappear. If you have to leave the meeting, let people know that you are disengaging. In smaller meetings, inform the entire group. If you know you will have to depart, let the group know beforehand that you will be leaving before the end of the meeting. In larger groups, you should advise the leader at your location that you must go.

THE BOTTOM LINE

➤ The basic rules of meeting courtesy apply to virtual meetings, even when participants are not in the same room.

➤ Ample preparation and rehearsal time is critical to successful facilitation of a virtual meeting.

➤ Have a plan for keeping everyone engaged and involved.

➤ Because of the distortions and amplifications caused by your screen presence, facilitators and participants should avoid wearing stripes and shiny jewelry, gesturing with big movements, and speaking too fast.

➤ Distractions are even more tempting when you are not physically present among meeting participants; make the effort required to pay attention, ignore incoming e-mails, and avoid side-conversations.

CHAPTER 22

How to Leave a Job

Making a Graceful Exit

*F*ew situations pose a greater challenge to flawless execution than leaving a job. Whatever the reason—your choice or not—your interpersonal skills and self-discipline will be put to the test. Leaving a job involves many of the feelings of separation and loss that accompany ending any close relationship. It's a time of stress when feelings and emotions run high, and you need to make sure that they don't run away with you. People around you will be observing your behavior, which can make a lasting impression on everyone around you; therefore, be sure that you exit with class.

LEAVING GRACEFULLY

People leave jobs for a variety of reasons, and although some general guidelines apply in any situation, some circumstances call for somewhat different departure strategies or special actions.

If You've Been Fired

Receiving a pink slip is a devastating experience for even the most self-confident person. We have a difficult time separating what we do from who we are, so losing a job for behavior or job performance reasons cuts to the core as a major rejection. We feel attacked, even if we know down deep that the company is on firm ground in taking action, and may want to lash out in self-defense. However, this situation demands a calm, rational approach to what is happening.

Analyze the reasons for your firing. Was the job technically beyond your abilities? Did its requirements run counter to your personality? For example, if you are a shy, reserved person who prefers to pursue a task in an orderly, uninterrupted fashion and you have been in a job that requires aggressive telemarketing or cold-calling, your lack of success shouldn't come as a big surprise. At least you have the empirical evidence that will keep you from putting yourself in a similar situation in the future.

On the other hand, perhaps you lost your job because you couldn't resist the temptation to party with friends on work nights and never managed to get to work on time in the morning, until your tardiness and absenteeism became intolerable to the department head.

Whatever the reason for your dismissal, look for what you can learn about yourself from this situation before you rush to blame the company or your supervisor. Mistakes can be great teachers and growth opportunities. If you're comfortable doing so, ask your former manager what changes you need to make in the future.

Even if the situation was not in any way your fault, and you got the axe to make room for the boss's nephew, you need to behave with dignity and grace. Express gratitude to your manager and others, if appropriate, for the opportunity to work at the company and mention some of the growth that you have experienced. Show appreciation to individual coworkers for their help and support during your tenure, and wish them the best in the future. Avoid making snide remarks about how you sympathize with them for having to continue working for Cruella de Vil and how you can't wait to find those greener pastures. Share any pertinent information you have that someone filling your position might need.

If you're angry, don't deny or smother your feelings, but find a venue outside your former workplace to vent. Avoid the temptation to rant on social media because you will end up looking like a whiner, and potential employers may see you as a loose cannon. Similarly, get your anger under control before you start to interview for another job. Alarms sound immediately in an interviewer's mind when an applicant makes negative remarks about a former employer.

If You're Laid Off

The principles of leaving after termination also apply in the event of a corporate downsizing in which you find yourself the unfortunate recipient of a layoff. Unlike being fired, which in most cases targets an individual, layoffs often involve a number of people who are leaving the company at the same time. Companies often go out of their way to make this kind of exit more palatable, sometimes allowing workers to maintain e-mail addresses and voice mailboxes along with providing them with outplacement counseling and coaching. Particularly in these circumstances, you don't want to burn any bridges because companies frequently rehire laid-off workers (if they're available) when conditions improve, or they may engage them on a contract or consulting basis.

The fact that others share your circumstances is emotionally comforting and can create a helpful support structure during a difficult time. You can be a vast source of networking and lead generation for each other. However, be sure that you don't turn the supportive network of fellow laid-off employees into a forum for grumbling and company bashing—before and after your actual separation from the company. Misery loves company, but such an environment can quickly poison your attitude in a way that may taint your job search.

If You *Choose* to Leave

In many cases, the decision to leave a company is your own and comes as the result of a better opportunity. If you find yourself in this situation, take the necessary steps to handle your departure with the poise that will leave everyone with a favorable impression.

First of all, put your resignation on paper. This letter is the permanent record for both the company and for the person who is leaving. The letter must be unemotional and factual only. You don't need to apologize or explain why you are leaving, although thanking the recipient for the opportunity to work there is appropriate. Primarily, the written record should include only the fact that you intend to leave and the effective date. Of course you will date and sign your letter. Atlanta-based Gayle Oliver, CEO of Execume, Inc., agrees with the concept of the formal letter but suggests that you call a face-to-face meeting in which you hand the letter across the table.

Occasionally, people who resign get a counteroffer to entice them to stay. Rarely, however, do people who rescind their resignation end up glad they did so. You have to wonder, after all, why, if you are so valuable to your current company, they didn't give you the recognition and reward before you resigned?

Thank the person who makes you the counteroffer, but assure him or her that you intend to honor your commitment to the new company. If you resigned just to spur your current employer into offering you more money or responsibility, no one will end up well-served and the company you used as a pawn in the match will never forgive you.

On the other hand, if the counteroffer seems too good to pass up, have a face-to-face conversation with your "almost" employer explaining exactly why you have changed your mind and decided to stay where you are. If you have already made a commitment to the new company, however, consider the possible consequences of reneging on an agreement, and do not, under any circumstances, allow yourself to get into a bidding war.

What follows the formal announcement to your supervisor depends on the policy of the company. In some cases, security will immediately meet you outside the manager's office and escort you, first back to your work space to gather your personal belongings and then out of the building.

If you work for a company that doesn't have someone escort you out the door immediately, but actually wants you to stay around for the time you set forth in your notice, here are a few guidelines to help you through the challenging process.

Try to leave on good terms with everyone. Although you might feel better for a few moments, resist the urge to unload on a coworker who may have made your life miserable. After all, people have been known to return to a former company, and you want to create as much goodwill as you can. If you have had difficulties with colleagues, find a way to smooth those relationships before you are gone forever. Thank everyone who helped you do your job or who showed you the ropes when you first joined the company. Be specific about what their guidance and support meant to you.

On the other hand, don't overpromise to stay in touch. Many of your associations with coworkers stem from the bond of working together. Once that connection no longer exists, you may not maintain an interest in continuing the relationships.

Jean Ann Cantore, editor of *Texas Techsan* magazine in Lubbock, Texas, cautions against making promises to come back to visit often or to help coworkers get a job with the new company. Not delivering on promises can seriously damage your credibility.

If you do stay connected to former coworkers, avoid digging for work-related dirt or gossip when you see or talk to them. You aren't an insider anymore, and people may not feel comfortable if you pry into information that should stay within the company.

Resist the urge to boast about your new position. If you are leaving for a better opportunity, avoid telling everyone how great your new company is. Be upbeat, but keep your enthusiasm under control. Avoid gloating over the big salary or the fabulous benefits package. You won't gain anything by encouraging others to leave, either. What's right for you may not be right for them. Even if the situation you are leaving is difficult for others also, don't make them feel bad about staying. They may not have the option.

Help ensure a smooth transition. Cantore also warns against assuming the short-timer's attitude. Put the same high level of energy into your work on your last days as you did when you weren't planning to leave, and add to your daily duties a spirit of helping those who will stay and have to deal with the issues of your transition. Share information about projects on which you were working. If others will be taking up the slack while the company looks for someone to replace you, make sure that you leave instructions about how to access the information they need. If your replacement is already on board, help him or her get up to speed.

Leave your work area and files organized and in good condition. You don't want to undo your former coworkers' good memories of you when they start picking up your unfinished projects.

After your departure, be available to answer any questions by phone or e-mail. You certainly can specify the best time to contact you at your new workplace. And although you obviously can't spend an inordinate amount of time during working hours coaching former coworkers or your replacement, you can save everyone grief by being a temporary resource as the former workplace learns to get along without you.

THE LAST IMPRESSION

Overall, the key to leaving employment is to exit with class. Treat this interaction as you would if it were your first encounter with the company, because this last impression you make will be the one your former employer will remember. You never know when the contacts you made there will pay big dividends or become a valuable resource. When people remember you, make sure they remember someone of the utmost integrity and professionalism.

THE BOTTOM LINE

> ➤ Leaving a work situation involves many of the feelings of separation and loss that accompany ending a close relationship.

> ➤ Keep your emotions under control, especially if you have bad feelings about the job you're leaving.

> ➤ Don't boast about the new position you are taking.

> ➤ Remember that the contacts you made at your former job can be valuable resources, so exit with class.

CHAPTER 23

Refuse to Schmooze and You Lose

Cultivating the Social Side of Business

A talented young woman in a fast-growing software development firm was shocked when her coworkers ranked her low in a peer-rated performance review. The reason? One recurring criticism was that she rarely socialized with other members of the company, never joining them for lunch or drinks after work and seldom attending company parties. They essentially saw her behavior as undermining the teamwork necessary to meet their corporate goals. "But I do great work," she lamented. "I didn't realize that being a party animal was part of the job description. And I'm just not good at that sort of thing!"

Do we really have to mix business and pleasure to make it in today's business environment? Must we be socially skilled as well as subject matter experts?

Like it or not, in today's climate of mergers and takeovers, downsizings and reorganizations, schmoozing, or the art of connecting with others in both business and social relationships, has become an imperative for career survival. Too many Boomers, Gen Xers, and Millennials are competing for a limited number of plum slots in both the public and private sectors. Furthermore, the number of management positions continues to shrink as companies trim costs and consolidate. With so many equally talented people in the workforce, and more on the horizon, those who understand the importance of relationships will outpace those who believe that refusing to play office "politics" is somehow a virtue.

PROFESSIONAL, NOT ANTISOCIAL

Being competent and professional does not mean that you're exempt from building rapport with your colleagues. In fact, if you fail to network, within your company and with clients, you'll find yourself lagging behind as coworkers move ahead. Making connections with key people is as vital a part of your career plan as being up-to-date on the latest development in your field or achieving your sales targets. Here are some tips that can help you be a better socializer, even if you don't have a natural affinity for it.

Keep your purpose firmly in mind. Whether it's a networking luncheon, an association meeting of people in your field, or the company picnic, if you have a purpose for attending, the prospect will seem less onerous and the event will be more rewarding. One reason that many people don't enjoy these business/social events is that they have no clear sense of why they're there. Often, people attend a particular company event just because they know that they are expected to go. Whatever your reason for attending, you can use the occasion to accomplish a goal of initiating new relationships or developing existing ones.

Set a goal, for example, of meeting three new people at the next professional organization networking event. Or perhaps you may go with the idea of making a contact with a particular person. For example, if you sell real estate and you keep hearing about a major competitor's top agent and you find out she's going to be there, make it a point to introduce yourself. Compliment her on her success; perhaps you will lay the groundwork for future collaboration—or at least you may pick up some tips.

Regardless of the contacts you meet, consider it an opportunity to make a worthwhile connection. Whenever you greet someone, make an effort to commit the person's name to memory. One trick is to use a person's name at least three times in the first two or three minutes. Also find out something about the person's job. If you exchange business cards, after a conversation, jot down a couple of comments that will help you remember something about the person. (For example, "In a new job. Knows Joan Kurshner.") When you return to your office, follow up with a short note or e-mail to help the people you met remember you, if you should decide to contact them again later. Put them in your contacts list so that reconnecting will be convenient.

If you are at a company party, use the social aspect of the occasion to step outside the normal corporate hierarchy. You may have always wanted to get to know the vice president of production a bit better, but your job or the pecking order doesn't allow daily interaction. Here is a great chance to initiate a relationship. If you know that he enjoys fly-fishing and it's also your passion, you have an instant conversation starter. Don't forget to include the spouses or partners of your coworkers, either. Take time to talk with them as well. They may feel a bit uncomfortable and will appreciate someone taking the time to chat for a moment. And they may pass on a compliment about you later.

Work the room. Nervousness and uncertainty in a social setting also can stem from the absence of a clear goal. Develop a plan. Arrive early and check out the surroundings. If it's buffet, eat first. Not only will you avoid the difficulties of shaking hands while balancing a plate and glass, but you will also be able to recommend something wonderful on the menu to a late arrival. Note the locations of the rest rooms or the bar that's out of the main traffic area. If you see someone who needs some direction, it's always a good way to start a conversation. Seek out people you would like to speak to, and make an effort to connect with them. Your associates will understand if you let them know what you're doing. For example, you might explain, "I'm going to try to talk to Ms. Martino while I'm here. I've been trying to get an appointment with her for six months."

Even if the idea of "working a room" seems scary at first, remember that you're at the event to socialize and meet people.

If it is a couple's event, explain to your spouse, date, or partner beforehand what you are trying to accomplish and how this occasion may give you the opportunity to make some headway professionally. Properly briefed, the person who comes with you may be a real asset or may prefer to mix and mingle independently. Letting your guest in on the strategy will also keep him or her from feeling abandoned if you step away to talk to someone.

Master the art of small talk. When you go to a social function, arrive prepared to talk to people. Catch up on the latest news before you go. What two or three stories grab your interest? Have some comments or opinions ready or some little-known fact about the event that everyone may not have heard. If the occasion includes a guest speaker, find out something about the speaker's work. Even the history of the building where the occasion is taking place or the chef who prepared the food may provide topics of conversation.

Act as a catalyst—help others to socialize. Be on the lookout for people who aren't talking to anyone and include them in your conversation. Draw other people into the discussion with connectors such as, "Lindsay, this is José. He just moved here from Tulsa. José, Lindsay grew up in Tulsa."

SCHMOOZING: MORE THAN JUST PARTIES

If parties just aren't your cup of tea, you have many other opportunities to schmooze that don't involve organized events. I once knew an executive who kept a list of all his employees' birthdays and sent each one of them a card that arrived on the day—a small gesture, but one that everyone appreciated. Be alert for ways to celebrate with people or express sympathy for their sorrow. I keep a collection of all-occasion cards in my office so that when I hear of a situation, I can respond appropriately and in a timely manner.

Another great way to network is to share topics of interest with people you know or would like to connect with, or to send copies of articles or pictures featuring them. Jot a short congratulatory or other suitable note on the article. Having it laminated before you send it is a nice touch.

Another networking trick some people use is keeping a filled candy dish on their desk and making it available to everyone. A computer company executive who was new to a particular office kept a doll in his office that dispensed candy when you shook its hand. The word spread quickly, and people from the entire office enjoyed dropping by for a treat—giving him an excellent opportunity to get to know his associates. Similarly, a woman at a large marketing organization became an information resource for her coworkers, thereby making herself known to everyone in her office. If anyone needed a painter, a paperhanger, a mechanic, a dentist, or a florist, she had the scoop.

IT'S ALL ABOUT RELATIONSHIPS

Schmoozing is not rigid adherence to a set of prescribed actions. It's a professional style that grows out of a genuine interest in others and a willingness to connect with them. How you choose to schmooze depends on your personality and your lifestyle—and it must be a fit for both if it's going to work. Otherwise, you'll come across as artificial, manipulative, and self-serving.

Done correctly, schmoozing will increase your sense of belonging and enable you to increase your own confidence and enrich the experiences of others.

THE BOTTOM LINE

> ➤ In today's business climate, schmoozing, or the art of connecting with others in both business and social relationships, has become an imperative for career survival.

> ➤ Set goals for social events just as you do for business situations.

> ➤ Mastering the art of small talk can make you and others feel at ease in unfamiliar surroundings.

> ➤ Schmoozing doesn't take place only at parties.

> ➤ Schmoozing becomes easier when it's based on a genuine regard for others.

CHAPTER 24

Let's Do Lunch

Dining Your Way to Success

$\mathcal{S}$ ince the first cave dweller decided to share rather than fight over that rack of mastodon, people have been breaking bread and raising their glasses as a way to develop and nurture relationships. Among other things, dining together implies a heightened level of trust, dating back to when warriors or nobles poured a little wine into each other's goblet to ensure that no poison was afoot. Today we just clink glasses in a symbolic gesture of confidence in the other's goodwill.

In the world of business, meals are often an essential element in conducting certain kinds of business, and knowing how to navigate gracefully around this maze of menus, manners, and maître d's can make a significant contribution to your personal and professional success.

Before you send that e-mail inviting a client, customer, or colleague to lunch, however, you need to answer some key questions: Does the purpose of the meeting suit a dining atmosphere? Is it a worthwhile investment of your time and your guest's time? Can you block enough of your schedule to be a gracious host or guest?

Although a business meal can be a great way to go off campus and conduct a conversation away from the normal interruptions of an office, not every business discussion lends itself to dining. Advancing a relationship to the next level, thanking someone for a job well done, taking one last look at a job candidate, or asking for support on a charitable fund drive are all legitimate business meal scenarios. On the other hand, any meeting that requires sticky negotiations, focuses on a sensitive or antagonistic issue, or calls for reams of paper spread across a table won't work in a typical restaurant setting. You can always have coffee and snacks available in your conference room when the situation demands an office environment, and box lunches are not just for picnics anymore but a familiar part of the office environment

WHEN YOU ARE THE HOST

However, if you decide that a business meal is appropriate, the experience can be a great way to build or strengthen professional relationships. Of course, if, as the host, you handle the situation with a lack of finesse, you might accomplish just the opposite. Here are a few guidelines to keep in mind.

Location, location, location. Whether the occasion will be festive or forgettable depends largely on the restaurant. When inviting a guest to join you for a meal, choose a place you know well. Save your adventurous dining impulses for the weekend dinner with friends and stick with the familiar for business dining. That way, you'll know that you can afford it, that it's quiet enough for you to talk comfortably, and that you will have enough distance between tables that you won't be distracted by the conversations of others or be concerned about privacy for your own discussion. I once took clients out to a business lunch only to end up in rather close quarters adjacent to a table where a man was asking his wife for a divorce. Needless to say, no one at our table could concentrate on anything but the unfortunate drama in progress.

Pick a place that accepts reservations and offers either valet or easily accessible parking, in case of bad weather. It's a good idea to keep a list of reliable favorite restaurants on hand, in case you draw a blank in the midst of issuing an invitation. In some cases, suggest two options, and allow your guest to choose.

Pay attention to timing. If you're taking someone to lunch, suggest a time other than noon, when the crowd hits. A 1:00 p.m. appointment allows you and your guest to complete a full morning's work and be ready for a more relaxed meal.

If time is an ongoing concern for you or your guest, consider a breakfast meeting. Many executives prefer to avoid a two-hour break in the middle of the day. Breakfast meetings usually last no more than an hour, cost considerably less than lunch or dinner, and don't interrupt the workday. Inviting someone to breakfast also says that you are a real go-getter who is up and out early.

Give your guest all necessary information. Provide directions, your mobile number, and a phone number for the restaurant if your guest isn't familiar with the location. Confirm with your guest the morning of the appointment (the afternoon before if it's breakfast) and arrive ten minutes early, so your guest doesn't have to wait for you, wondering if it's the right place. If you are expecting more than one guest, be seated with the first guest after waiting for at least ten minutes for the late arrival.

Know also that as the person who extended the invitation, you pay the bill, as well as fees or tips for parking and checking coats. Men should become comfortable allowing a female business associate to pay for the meal, even though they might not do so in a social situation. Indicating to your server that you want the other person(s) to order first lets the server know who will be picking up the check.

The reason I called this meeting . . . Although the purpose of a business meeting is, obviously, to discuss a business topic, having the meeting over a meal introduces a social element. Therefore, there must be a balance between the business focus and the social aspects of the gathering. Avoid talking any business until the server has taken everyone's order. As the person who initiated the occasion, you should make a smooth transition from small talk to business. If the meal is dinner, keep the business conversation to a minimum, perhaps as late in the meal as dessert and coffee. On the other hand, since breakfast meetings are often shorter, you may begin discussing business once everyone receives the first cup of coffee or tea.

If you're the host, your job is to make sure that the dialogue stays focused and pleasant. Manage the emotions of the group and use your voice and body language to keep things under control. Never raise your voice to a level that people around you can hear your conversation.

Handle interruptions with poise. If you see a friend or acquaintance in the restaurant, a simple greeting is sufficient. If that person stops at your table, introduce him or her to the others at the table and say that it's been a pleasure to see that person. Don't engage in a lengthy conversation, and don't ask the person to join you. Further-more, you shouldn't table-hop and interrupt others' discussions.

If you must make a phone call during the meal, leave the table to do so. Keep your mobile phone turned off unless you're expecting a call critical to the matter at hand. If you're so busy that you can't be unhooked for an hour, use the drive-through at Big Burger for lunch.

Mind your manners. Although our society grows ever more casual, many of our remaining civilizing rituals revolve around table manners. Here are a couple of key rules to remember:

- ➤ Place your napkin in your lap *as soon as everyone is seated.* If you leave the table during the meal, leave your napkin in the chair, rather than to the left of your plate. A used napkin is unattractive and unsanitary.

- ➤ Cutlery is arranged so that you use the piece farthest away from the plate first. If you have to leave the table and you don't want your plate removed, place the knife and fork in an "X" forma-tion across the plate, with the knife on the bottom and the fork on top, tines down. When you are finished and want your plate removed, place the knife and fork parallel to each other on the plate, with the handles at four o'clock and the tips at ten o'clock. Don't push your plate out of the way when you're finished. Let the server remove it.

IF YOU ARE THE GUEST

Whether you're the host or the guest at a business meal, many of the same rules apply. However, here are some additional rules to keep in mind.

Be courteous and considerate. When you are invited to a business meal, arriving on time shows professionalism and courtesy. Make every effort to arrive on time. If you arrive before your host, check to see if a reservation exists in your host's name; if the restaurant is becoming crowded, ask the greeter to seat you and then direct others to your table.

Conversely, if you are quite late and others have started without you, begin your order with whatever course is in process. Never order the most expensive item on the menu, and don't order anything alcoholic if no one else is drinking. If they are and you wish to order, one drink should be your limit at a lunch meeting.

If for any reason you can't keep the appointment, call the person who invited you *yourself*. Don't have someone do it for you, and don't leave the message on voice mail.

WHEN ALL IS SAID AND DONE

If you were the guest at a business meal, a short thank-you note is a particularly thoughtful way to express your appreciation to your host. However, a phone call or an e-mail is better than no thanks at all. If you were the host, evaluate the occasion to determine if you accomplished your purpose or if another arena might have been more comfortable or productive.

Think of a business meal as a sizable investment, not an antidote to brown bag blues. Whether you are host or guest, you share the responsibility for making that investment pay big dividends for everyone.

THE BOTTOM LINE

- ➤ Dining out is a great way to build rapport and conduct appropriate kinds of business.
- ➤ Rules of conduct apply to everyone in any business dining situation.
- ➤ Understand the specific protocol for the guest and the host, and be sure to fulfill those particular obligations

CHAPTER 25

Getting Noticed—
Without Becoming Notorious

I'm fine in one-on-one situations," lamented a coaching client. "But I can go to a company meeting or a conference, and no one remembers that I was even there. It's like I'm invisible," he said, adding, "I have great relationships with people after they get to know me."

His situation is not unusual. Although many of us have little trouble relating to the people who know us well, we often can't seem to get a handle on how to make sure we get noticed and remembered in a group or during brief encounters. Particularly in business, an immediate and lasting positive impression can make the difference between success and failure—whether during a job interview, in a meeting with the department head, or when meeting potential clients.

A PROACTIVE APPROACH

Some people can thank genetics for their ability to get noticed. They may be stunningly good-looking or unusually tall, for example, or they may be naturally gregarious, having no trouble connecting with people in any situation. On the other hand, some people tend to be memorable for all the wrong reasons. These people may come across as eccentric or obnoxious. Most of us, however, fall in the "ordinary" category. If you're one of these people, that doesn't mean that you can't stand out in a crowd. You don't have to be a creative genius or have a charismatic personality to become a star both socially and on the job. A little planning can go a long way toward putting you in the spotlight.

Make sure that you always look your best. Business casual notwithstanding, you still need to look rested, immaculately groomed, and well put together. Know the colors that support your natural coloring and avoid those that make you look washed out, tired, or overpowered. In addition to making others take you more seriously, knowing that you look great will give you added assurance and make you behave with more confidence.

Make the first move. Don't wait for people to approach you to start a conversation. Engage people with confidence, and extend your hand for a handshake. Involve others in a conversation about a relevant topic, such as the event you're attending or exciting news in your industry. Also, if you know something about the person to whom you are speaking, be prepared to talk about a subject that interests him or her.

When you see a new business acquaintance again, don't hang back and wait for the other person to speak to you. Make the first move, and always mention your name immediately, to avoid embarrassing the person if he or she doesn't remember it. It's also a good idea to remind people where you met previously so that they can make the necessary mental connections.

Use questions to your advantage. People enjoy talking about themselves, so a good conversation starter would be a question about the person's career or field. For example, ask questions such as, "How did you get started with the company?" "What trends do you see in your field?" or "What do you think are the most formidable challenges ahead of us at Cyberworks?" Usually, you can then stand back and let the other person guide the conversation. People will remember your interest in them and your knowledge of what they find intriguing.

GET NOTICED AT WORK

Star performers all share certain characteristics, even though their personal styles may differ dramatically. The people who stand out from the pack understand how the office works and navigate office politics effectively. Here are some basic rules.

Avoid taking sides or alienating anyone. If things around the office are tense and divisive because of conflicts among other people, stay out of any disagreements. Seek the guidance of a mentor with the experience and wisdom to steer you through this and other tricky situations.

Show initiative. Go beyond the requirements or the bare minimum. People who solve problems and get involved in projects without worrying if those tasks are part of their job descriptions are bound to get positive recognition sooner or later. When possible, volunteer to tackle those little tasks that no one seems to have time for but that are not too large to interfere with your regular duties. It pays to become known as a "get it done" person.

In meetings, speak early and comment often. Even if you just ask a question, make yourself heard to show that you are participating actively. However, don't overdo it, because then it will appear that you are speaking up to stand out and not because you have anything of value to say. Bob Nelson, author of, *1001 Ways to Take Initiative at Work,* calls it the "Three-F Rule." Speak *fast* enough to convey a sense of importance and urgency. Speak *fluently* enough to come across as comfortable and in control. And speak *forcefully* enough to show that you believe in what you're saying.

Present ideas that can benefit others. When you have an idea that may benefit your department or the company (or a coworker or the boss, for that matter), share it. Your suggestions don't have to be revolutionary; they may be small ways to serve customers better, boost productivity or morale, or make a job easier.

Think and speak strategically, with long-term benefits in mind. Eleanor Roosevelt said, "Great minds discuss ideas; average minds discuss events; small minds discuss people." Elevate the conversation with a plan to solve a problem or implement a procedure. People who constantly raise issues without ever having a solution quickly become tiresome and ineffective.

Don't fear self-promotion. You may feel uncomfortable asserting yourself or making people aware of your talents and abilities. But, as the old saying goes, if it's a fact, it isn't bragging. Don't assume that just doing a good job will get you noticed. In today's highly competitive, information-overloaded, speed-of-light environment, reluctance to make sure that you get the right kind of attention can be damaging in the long run and rob you of the opportunity to reap the recognition and the rewards that you deserve. When the occasion presents itself, mention some specific accomplishments that are relevant to the topic being discussed and that focus on the benefits of your actions to the company or others.

THE BOTTOM LINE

➤ An immediate and lasting positive impression can make the difference between success and failure.

➤ Take a proactive approach to getting noticed.

➤ A little planning can go a long way toward putting you in the spotlight at work.

➤ Present ideas that can benefit others—and the company.

➤ Don't be afraid of self-promotion as long as it doesn't damage or denigrate others.

CHAPTER 26

He Said, She Said

When the Gender Gap Seems as Wide as the Grand Canyon

*S*everal decades of debate and wrangling about the differences between the sexes have yielded at least one area on which most members of both sexes can agree: Gender has nothing to do with a person's ability to do a job, but men and women *are* different. But you already knew that, didn't you? Conversational, problem-solving, and decision-making styles, although certainly unique to individuals, often exhibit themselves in certain discernible patterns according to gender.

The more you understand some of those differences, the less inclined you'll be to react negatively when you confront them in stressful situations.

MEN AND WOMEN REALLY *ARE* DIFFERENT

A huge body of work exists on this subject, and theories abound about the source of these differences. Deborah Tannen, author of *You Just Don't Understand: Women and Men in Conversation,* is a leading authority on the topic. Tannen points out that even though we all agree that generalizing and stereotyping are largely demonized in our society, there is truth to some of the generalizations about gender and communications. Furthermore, our ability to understand and classify patterns of behavior helps us move past the generalizations and opens the door to a workable method for addressing differences in behavior and creating stronger working and personal relationships.

Just about everyone at one time or another has lived with a member of the opposite sex—whether a parent, sibling, partner, spouse, or roommate. As a result of these experiences, we can all share some of the humorous and frustrating approaches to the world around us that emanate from the other gender. And we have, on occasion, been befuddled and frustrated by our seeming inability to communicate with each other. It's often enough to make us think that we come from different planets.

Experts hypothesize about whether these differences are biological, environmental, or both. But instinctively, most of us know that, beginning in the nursery, men and women have been dealt with and treated differently. Their parents talk to them differently and expect disparate conversation from them. And, as they begin to socialize, children interact with others in contrasting manners. According to Tannen, boys tend to play outside, in large groups, with a distinctly structured hierarchy, consisting of a leader who expects to have his position challenged regularly. Girls play in smaller groups, in less competitive activities, where everyone takes a turn and no one necessarily wins or loses.

As adults in the workplace, grown-up boys and girls still struggle with or seek to leverage these differences. Tannen points out that women's communication often aims at intimacy while men's interactions and communication styles have to do with establishing status. For example, even today, many women may still downplay their accomplishments in order to avoid resentment and perhaps ostracism. Men, on the other hand, make sure that others recognize their accomplishments, in order to gain their respect.

The fact that women like to talk isn't just a myth. A 2006 study discovered that women talk about three times as much as men in a given day, with the average woman chalking up 20,000 words in a day—13,000 more than the average man, who speaks around 7,000 words.

BRIDGING THE GENDER DIVIDE

What can we do to bridge the chasm that sometimes demands huge amounts of energy to deal with and creates more than a little dissension, which can interfere with productivity and sabotage morale? Perhaps a few reminders for understanding the differences between the genders can create a more harmonious and synergistic workplace where everyone benefits.

Recognize potential differences in conversational styles.

> *"She started telling me about a problem, and I offered what I thought was a perfectly good solution. It seemed to make her angry."*
>
> *"He always seems impatient when I try to explain something. He keeps interrupting me, telling me to get to the point."*
>
> *"Why can't she just tell me the facts without making it sound like a soap opera?"*
>
> *"A simple thank you would be nice."*

These comments, and many like them, stem from our bewildered reactions to differences that often occur when men and women communicate. Recognizing inherent communication differences and using what we learn to accommodate each other and avoid strife in the workplace can help us to appreciate the many ways we are alike.

In a typical conversation, men state their ideas, opinions, and requests directly, using few words and little reliance on an emotional appeal. Women, on the other hand, will use conversation to build relationships and to connect with others. Jane Thomas, author of the *Guide to Managerial Persuasion and Influence,* notes that women often use questions to keep the conversation flowing while men use questions as simply requests for information. Whereas a man will more often tend toward advocacy of ideas, women frequently employ the technique of inquiry to create a collaborative environment and gain input from others.

When dealing with issues or problems, women habitually like to describe the situation as a way of either venting about the subject or organizing their thoughts while talking. On the other hand, when presented with a problem, men feel the need to go into a "fix it" mode immediately, or they interpret the complaint as a personal attack. For example, if a female coworker stops at a male coworker's desk and says, "The copier was out of paper—again," the man's response may be, "Well, it's not my job to keep it stocked." In reality, the woman is probably not telling the man because she thinks it's his fault. She just wants someone to show sympathy for her frustration and inconvenience.

In meetings, presentations, or classrooms, women nod and smile—encouraging and supporting the conversation without necessarily agreeing with the content. Men sit there, often expressionless and without making eye contact, taking an occasional note, yet suddenly their comment or response reveals that they are totally engaged in the discussion.

Identify and accommodate yourself to your audience's needs. As in any communication situation, effectiveness increases when each party makes an effort to give the other party what he or she needs. In *Gender Games*, Candy Tymson offers the following advice for workplace communication.

FOR MEN
➤ Avoid dominating conversations.
➤ Refrain from interrupting.
➤ Remember to use "please" and "thank you" when directing, ordering, or requesting.

FOR WOMEN
➤ Don't dilute your comments with phrases such as "Isn't it?" or "Don't you think?"
➤ Avoid inserting too much personal information into conversations; rather, focus on job-related topics.
➤ Promote yourself, when appropriate, by letting others know of your achievements.

Be aware of potential differences in nonverbal communication. Although we all communicate through body language, eye contact, and gestures, certain types of nonverbal communication seem to be favored by either men or women. Typically, women tend to smile more, stare less, use touch to express support and comfort, and send a lot of messages with their facial expressions.

Conversely, men characteristically maintain more reservation and control of their facial expressions, although they may gesture more. Men tend to use more personal space than women and often are accused of invading others' space, particularly if the "other" is female. (Think of the last time you were crammed into a crowded airplane. Who laid claim to the common armrest?)

If you're a woman, monitor your body language and facial expressions to avoid signaling agreement if you don't concur. And if you're male, make an effort to show your interest and attentiveness more actively. This can go a long way toward building productive associations and alliances.

Avoid mimicking the other gender's behavior. Being comfortable in your own skin (and that includes your own gender) is a key part of being a competent, credible, and mature adult. Studies show that when one gender seeks to take on the communication behaviors of the other, the results are less than satisfying. For example, a woman in business who tries to be "one of the boys" usually incurs resentment on both sides of the gender divide.

On the other hand, we're aware enough of gender differences by now to know that certain overarching behaviors really send the opposite sex up the wall, such as women's need to vent without closure and men's tendency to demand rather than request. Awareness combined with appropriate compensating behaviors can be useful in making sure that we minimize tendencies that can interfere with productive associations.

A genuine respect for people as individuals can help you accept differences. Remember that *different* doesn't mean superior or inferior. In fact, dissimilarities in perspectives regarding problem solving, decision making, and exploring ideas can result in increased creativity, better solutions, and higher-quality work products.

Bear in mind also that gender is merely one aspect of the diversity that informs our uniqueness as human beings. Distinctions in personal style, environment, education, and life experiences all play a part in our behavior and create divergences from what we might consider the norm. For example, although the norm for women is to couch observations or criticisms in neutral remarks, we've all known women who are blunt and bottom-line oriented. Similarly, while men in general communicate little through body language, there are men who nod, smile, and encourage during conversation.

When confronted with conduct that makes you uncomfortable, try to discover the intentions of the person whose behavior is disquieting. If other factors indicate that the person's motives are positive and respectful, it will be easier to get past the irritating behavior. For example, Bob may approach you speaking loudly and waving his arms, but after really listening to him, you may realize that his words are appropriate and not a personal attack aimed at you. Therefore, you might conclude that Bob is under stress and that his "outburst" is his response to the stress. Similarly, you may be bothered that Judith always wants to tell you what's going on in her life. But upon closer consideration, you may realize that she is trying to show you that she understands the pressure you're under and the compassion that she feels.

If you can recognize that often someone's behavior is more likely his or her reaction to a particular situation and not a personal attack, you will be in a much better position to deal with it and react appropriately. Although a certain degree of tolerance is admirable, you should be willing to push back if someone's behavior, whether from the opposite or same sex, infringes on your ability to make yourself heard and get your ideas across.

Understanding gender differences is merely a place to start as we sort out ways to improve our ability to communicate with each other. We have much to discover from other people, and removing barriers that prevent us from acquiring that important knowledge is always worth the effort.

THE BOTTOM LINE

- ➤ Differences in both verbal and nonverbal patterns often manifest themselves in intergender communication.
- ➤ Consciously mimicking the other gender's typical communication behaviors is rarely productive.
- ➤ Minimizing behaviors that negatively affect members of the opposite sex may facilitate communication and interaction.
- ➤ Genuine respect for people as individuals helps overcome personal style and other barriers.

CHAPTER 27

Citizenship in the Global Village

7 am not an Athenian or a Greek, but a citizen of the world." When Socrates uttered these words, the "world" was still a place with limited boundaries. He would be astounded today to see the extent to which our global citizenship has developed. Indeed, no one needs to tell you that globalization has occurred in our workplace, our businesses, our schools, and our neighborhoods.

Many good books tell us how we differ from our neighbors around the world in such social behaviors as eye contact, touch, the use of personal space, gestures, interactions with authority, and attitudes toward time. This chapter merely looks at some overall principles that may help you as you expand your horizons and come in contact with a growing number of people whose backgrounds and experiences differ from your own.

AVOIDING CROSS-CULTURAL COMMUNICATION PITFALLS

Those who began their lives with English as our native language can take some comfort in the fact that English is currently considered the international language of business, thanks to the far-flung influence of the British Empire and its extensive colonization pursuits. Many of us in the English-speaking world lag behind the rest of the population in our ability to speak more than one language, whereas for a huge number of people in the world, English is a second, third, or even fourth language, enabling efficiencies in doing business.

The English language incorporates a wide variety of usage, pronunciation, and meanings even among those who speak it as their native tongue. And although we can't solve all the problems that English presents to non-native speakers, we can be mindful of our use of words and remember that three key areas present particular opportunities for confusion or frustration: idioms, jargon/acronyms, and humor.

The Idiom Trap

Idioms are those expressions common to the language that can't be literally translated, such as "We're in the ballpark," "I'll keep tabs on the situation," "She let the cat out of the bag," "He's on cloud nine," and "Let's touch base tomorrow." Someone with a language-to-language dictionary would find it futile to put the individual elements of these phrases together and make any sense out of them.

While conducting an introductory exercise during one of my workshops several years ago, I asked participants to find out a number of facts about each other, one of which was someone's "pet peeve." I discovered, to my chagrin, that the international participants were unfamiliar with the term. I should have known better, but my mistake illustrates the quandary that presents itself in communicating cross-culturally.

As native speakers of English, we become so accustomed to these phrases that we fail to see them as anything other than everyday expressions that our common experience has made ordinary and mutually understood. The new global arena requires that we step back and become sensitive to these colorful but potentially perplexing phrases. At the very least, it's helpful to have a quick concise definition that familiarizes the audience with the meaning.

The Jargon Jumble

Jargon presents another obstacle to the non-native speaker who is trying to understand English. Today's business environment is full of jargon such as "bottom line" and "bells and whistles." We've taken a fancy to turning nouns into verbs, so we "effort" to accomplish something, "task" someone with an assignment, or "dialogue" about a problem. In some companies, particular departments or professions have their own language so that even talking across functions can be challenging. And that doesn't even start to deal with the overabundance of acronyms that infuse most organizations today. Jargon is a kind of useful shorthand that lets colleagues know that you have expertise in a particular area. In fact, a facility with industry or corporate lingo can enhance your credibility. Using jargon works fine as long as everyone knows the code. Make sure that you are confident that when you use jargon you are using it around people who understand what you mean. If you have the slightest doubt, translate the term into plain language.

Humor—Not Funny in All Languages

Remember also that humor doesn't always translate seamlessly, and even if it does, different cultures find different things amusing—or not. Poking fun or playing a practical joke on someone who is working through unfamiliar surroundings may result in humiliation or anger. Or a joke may just fall flat because the listener doesn't "get it" because of trouble with translation or different values.

Being sensitive doesn't mean that you have to give up having fun or keep your communication solemn. Just watch for reactions, explain when necessary, apologize if you offend, and avoid issues that you know will be problematic.

Other Cultural Hurdles

Here are some additional guidelines that will help you when talking with those from another country.

Be aware of your unspoken message. Nonverbal communication can be confusing even when everyone shares a similar cultural experience. Our words and our nonverbal signals may be at odds, for example. We might say "yes" but our body language says "no." The nonverbal components vary markedly from culture to culture. For example, is it appropriate to make eye contact or not? Is touching someone okay or taboo? What's the proper distance between you and the other person in a conversation? Knowing the answers to these and similar questions can mean the difference between connecting with and offending a peer from a different background.

Remember that gestures are particularly tricky. In some cultures, for instance, nodding the head means "no" or "I heard you," rather than "yes" or "I agree." Forming a circle with the thumb and forefinger, which means "Okay" in the United States, has a variety of meanings around the world—from the obscene to signifying money.

If another person's friendly gesture is your insult, explain what the gesture means in your own culture. Avoid being derogatory but merely point out the differences in the use of that particular custom. Not only will your explanation ease the immediate tension but it will also help that person in future encounters.

Understand that not everyone craves the spotlight. In the United States, we generally want to stand out in the crowd. We glorify the "winners" in our society, in sports, entertainment, and business. Our celebrities command our attention, often for outrageous behavior. In much of the world, however, the team or group is more important than the individual, and drawing attention to oneself is not a virtue. One manager who wanted to praise an employee who did a particularly good job on a project found that his announcing her accomplishment in a department meeting produced a negative response from her. She later described his actions as humiliating and accused him of making a "spectacle" of her in front of her colleagues. She preferred to be a part of a successful team rather than to be an individual star. Understanding the differences between individualistic and collectivist cultures can help managers be successful in managing in a multicultural environment.

Show an interest in others' cultures. The more we know about each other, the less baffling and disturbing our respective differences in behavior appear. Encourage people with whom you work and relate to tell you about their way of life, customs, holidays and celebrations, and prohibitions. Sherron Bienvenu, president of the training and consulting firm Communication Solutions, notes that Americans have to work hard to dispel the "ugly American" stereotype. She suggests that people in the United States should make a special effort to find out how customs, procedures, and business practices differ in other countries, and when working with people from other cultures, either at home or abroad, we should remember to be sensitive to these differences in what they say and how they act.

Some companies encourage greater appreciation for diverse cultures by designating a day for sharing foods, explaining the significance of certain holidays, and engaging in roundtable discussions in which employees can learn more about each other. But real progress in understanding between people usually occurs in one-on-one situations.

Don't depend solely on institutionalized initiatives to help you cross a cultural gulf. Take it upon yourself to reach out to people of different backgrounds and, at the very least, to read about other cultures.

While most people will appreciate your interest in their customs, keep your inquiries broad-brushed and generic. Members of some cultures are uncomfortable with questions that seem to pry into their personal lives. And be sure to explain your reasons for asking questions. Show that you are genuinely interested and that you want to know more about their history, religion, or traditions.

Most people, however, are happy to talk about subjects that are familiar and important to them. Your willingness to listen in an appreciative and nonjudgmental way will make a significant impact on someone who may feel set apart and who may see you as a "stranger" or "foreigner."

Make sure that you adopt a position of inquiry rather than advocacy. Avoid creating a tit-for-tat situation in which you counter every statement or piece of information with a "This is how *we* do it" comeback. Let the speaker hold center stage unless he or she asks you about your own situation, and, as Bienvenu suggests, be patient. "Americans interrupt too easily," she notes. "When we understand the question, we jump to answer it. Most other cultures will wait patiently for the speaker to finish, and we should return that respect."

Avoid sending a message of cultural superiority. Being proud of our ethnic, national, religious, or racial origins is healthy and helps define who we are. Our self-esteem often connects closely with the communities in which we trace our roots . However, national or ethnic pride should not translate to arrogance or superiority (although we know that it often does). When you explain aspects of your culture, make sure that you do it in a way that informs rather than attempts to convert or persuade someone about the particular virtues of your own conventions.

Remember that different doesn't mean better or worse. Traditions usually develop because of a particular society or group's needs, given their circumstances and challenges, and we should accept rather than criticize those differences. Sharing should be descriptive rather than evaluative—a way to bring about awareness rather than to debate values. A genuine respect for others includes valuing cultural differences.

BECOMING A CONSTANT LEARNER

Companies today know that they must bridge cultural and language barriers in order for their organizations to succeed. Likewise, individuals who improve their intercultural savvy and lessen their tendency to ethnocentrism will enhance their acceptance by others.

Opportunities for learning abound. Members of corporations who are being sent to work in an office in another country have access to extensive training to alleviate much of the discomfort and uncertainty of working in an unfamiliar place. But even if you are working in your home country, you still have many occasions for strengthening relationships and reducing miscommunication and misunderstandings by taking the initiative to read, discuss, and observe. A colleague's refusal to partake of certain food at the company picnic may be based on a religious observance rather than a lack of appreciation for the event planners' efforts.

Understanding differences and points of similarity among us, as people of different cultures and backgrounds, can facilitate decision making, negotiations, and the way we conduct meetings and make commitments. The more we know about each other, the more we can become proficient at dealing with each other in an affirming way.

Remember also that cultures are dynamic. Just as your own society is constantly shifting and changing, so are others throughout the world. Keeping current, developing an inquisitive attitude, and continuing to conduct meaningful dialogue with those in neighboring cubicles or on the next continent will pay dividends in your own effectiveness and make doing business less difficult and more productive for everyone.

THE BOTTOM LINE

> ➤ Both our verbal and nonverbal messages create pitfalls in our intercultural interaction.

> ➤ In dealing with people from other cultures, show an interest and avoid any appearance of sending a message of cultural superiority.

> ➤ Bridging cultural and language barriers is essential for organizational and personal success in today's global marketplace.

PART 3

Handling Sensitive Issues: Courtesy and Building Trust

CHAPTER 28

Loving Your Enemies

Coping with the Price of Success

You worked nights, weekends, and holidays. You ate, slept, and breathed your job. And it finally paid off. Your promotion to vice president was announced last Monday.

After chairing the most successful charity ball in the city's history, your picture graces the cover of two local magazines this month.

You've been buried in the research department for three years, but now you're set to anchor the afternoon news next week.

Your division dragged through two years of lackluster performance, then you took the helm and made it the company's top performer.

These scenarios sound like a sure sign of having made it, right? Not necessarily. They might be an even surer sign of having made an enemy or two—people who resent your climb to stardom.

*W*hy is it so difficult to get to the top without making people around you angry and resentful? Part of it is just human nature. Years ago I heard a speaker comment that the English language has numerous words for expressing our sorrow for another person's pain—words like sympathy, empathy, pity, and compassion. But we don't have similar words to express feelings of joy for another's joy and success. Indeed, it's difficult for the "have-nots" to rejoice with the "haves." In fact, it's even hard for those who are among the "haves" to be happy for those who have *just a bit more.*

Furthermore, our society invariably cheers for the underdog. We worship our heroes on the way up: the baseball team that goes from worst to first; the unknown who comes out of nowhere to win the PGA tournament; the actress who wins an Oscar for her first film; the political novice who becomes president. Their associates and the public adore them all—for a while.

Although we're intrigued by an ascent to prominence, we also seem to want to create heroes only to tear them down. Once the rookie becomes a bona fide star, he or she also becomes fair game—not only for the media and every armchair critic, but also for teammates or colleagues who resent or feel threatened by that person's success. And social media allows just about anyone to spread rumors, criticize, and sabotage. In the same way, your own success may be tainted by enemies who seem to emerge out of nowhere to rain on your parade—from a snide remark here and there to an all-out campaign to bring you down.

MANAGING THE PRICE OF SUCCESS

How do you cope with this unfortunate price of success—without ending up looking like a spoiled, supersensitive whiner who can't take the glare of the spotlight?

First of all, identify the reason for the enmity. Enemies generally fall into two categories: those who may have good reason to dislike you and those who simply resent your success. The latter group, in some cases, may include people who do not even know you but consider you an appropriate target. In either case, some general guidelines may come in handy as you maneuver this tricky terrain.

Take an honest look at criticism. Once you get wind of someone's hostility toward you, whether it's firsthand or hearsay, take a moment to step back from your natural reaction of shock and hurt and ask yourself if what that person is saying is true. For example, have you been behaving narcissistically of late? Were you all too willing to take credit for a particular success without acknowledging others' contributions? If the painful reality is that you don't wear your crown with grace, other people's observations, however mean-spirited, may actually be a favor, because they give you the opportunity to look at yourself critically and identify changes you need to make in your behavior. In most cases, taking stock of our shortcomings every so often helps us to make progress toward development and maturity.

Clear the air. If the enemy seems to be a specific individual, try to put a lid on the person badmouthing you. Who is doing the talking? Is it someone who usually complains about everything and criticizes everyone, or are you the specific target? Is this person someone who seeks attention through controversy? Or is the hater someone you have wronged in some way, either deliberately or inadvertently? In either case, a calm, low-key conversation could be in order. Rather than listening to third-party reports, seek out the person in an arena that's nonthreatening to you both and talk about the issues.

In this kind of conversation, you'll be better off asking questions rather than making direct or accusing statements. Aim for closure. End the conversation with a discussion of what the two of you can do to get along better.

Deflate the issue with humor. It's easy to dislike a pompous and self-important person. On the other hand, it's difficult to maintain a grudge against a person who is the first to point out his or her own failings and to laugh at them. Successful politicians have learned well the lessons of criticizing themselves before someone else does.

And humor, particularly self-deprecating humor, can be engaging and can defuse a volatile situation. For example, if you're being accused of letting your success go to your head, turn the accusation into a joke: "Some of you have heard that I want a new chair for my office. The rumors are absolutely untrue that I'm shopping for a throne."

Take the high ground. When we've been hurt, the natural reaction is to defend ourselves using the same weapons as our opponent. If you are the one in power, however, retaliation in kind will make you look like a bully. Treat your attacker with respect, and avoid the temptation to tell the world how you really feel about the unfair treatment. In fact, if you say nothing but good things about those other people, their verbal assaults on or about you will begin to backfire.

Cut your losses. Come to terms with the fact that no matter how hard you try to avoid making enemies or no matter what you do to make amends, some people are still going to be jealous of you or just aren't going to like you. As painful as it may seem, the odds of a few personality clashes existing among 7 billion people are fairly high.

When all else fails, try to put a positive spin on your dilemma, at least in your own mind. After all, having an enemy or two attests to the fact that you have achieved something worthy of notice and, yes, envy. In a slightly perverse way, that's a surefire validation of your success.

THE BOTTOM LINE

- ➤ Getting to the top without causing resentment and jealousy is almost impossible.
- ➤ Most people invariably root for the underdog and like to tear down heroes.
- ➤ When faced with resentment, engage in some self-examination to make sure you aren't causing it.
- ➤ Use self-deprecating humor to soothe tensions.
- ➤ Work to defuse the conflict, but accept the fact you can't charm everyone.

CHAPTER 29

When Your Best Friend Becomes Your Boss

Balancing the Professional and the Personal

The two of you started working for the company at about the same time, learning the ropes and navigating the stormy seas of corporate politics. You shared each other's frustrations and victories and, over time, your professional relationship turned into a close friendship. You know each other's families, frequently visit in each other's homes, and have even taken an occasional family vacation together.

This morning, you sat in a department meeting as the company CEO announced your friend's promotion to department head. Now, in addition to being your friend, she's also your manager.

It's not just the office romance that can create a sticky situation in the workplace. Indeed, maintaining equilibrium between professional and personal relationships is never easy, even when friends work together as peers. How then do you work for your best friend and keep the integrity of the business relationship without destroying the friendship? Conversely, how do you maintain the friendship and not undermine both your careers as well as the company's business goals?

REINVENTING THE RULES OF FRIENDSHIP

When a workplace friend suddenly becomes your boss, the rules of the friendship must be reinvented for the office. If you find yourself in that situation, here are some basic guidelines to keep in mind.

Recognize that your working relationship is significantly changed. Even in organizations that adhere to an egalitarian philosophy, your friend is now your manager. The same rules that would govern any other two people in that situation apply to your new workplace relationship: You are now manager and direct report, and you must accord your friend the same respect you would give anyone else in that position, which means not taking liberties because the boss is your friend. For example, if you wouldn't go barging into another supervisor or manager's office, you shouldn't in this situation, either. Even if you formerly operated in a *mi cubicle es su cubicle* atmosphere, the boundaries are now different.

Rod Hewitt, vice president of human resources, Global Supply Chain at VF Corporation, comments on these sensitive workplace situations: "I think both people have to be conscious that there is now a supervisory/employee relationship. It's probably more important for the supervisor to make sure that both parties understand the relationship. The supervisor must be conscious that he or she is the ultimate decision maker, without being overbearing. The employee/friend should not to be scared to question ideas, but both people need to understand that the manager is ultimately responsible and accountable."

Even if your boss wants to maintain a certain social rapport in the office, use good judgment. If you routinely have coffee together first thing in the morning or if you habitually show up expecting to have lunch together, like in the old days, you will be perceived by coworkers, and perhaps even by your new boss, as taking unfair advantage of the situation.

Know that you and your manager are both under scrutiny. Your coworkers will be watching to see if you get special treatment. It's tempting for new managers to rely on people they know well and can trust. However, bosses who respond to employees according to their personal preferences, giving the plum assignments to their favorites and rewarding employees who flatter and bring good news, quickly lose credibility with their people. Furthermore, the recipient of that favor can suffer the wrath of those less favored and end up isolated and out of the loop. Therefore, know that signs of any favoritism will do neither you nor your new boss any good in the long term. Expect, and even demand, to be treated in the same way as everyone else.

At the other end of the spectrum, your new manager may be overly conscious of the implications of the friendship and treat you more sternly than the rest, giving others the key assignments and passing you by when promotion opportunities arise, for fear of being accused of favoritism.

If this situation occurs, you need to assess all the possible reasons for your manager's behavior. Take a hard, objective look at your skills and accomplishments. Is your supervisor trying too hard to be fair to the others, or has he observed something about you, over time, that has challenged his confidence in you? After you've done your own self-analysis, arrange for a meeting with your manager. Keep the meeting professional and unemotional and treat it like a job interview or performance review. Document your accomplishments, outline your goals, and press for an honest evaluation of your potential.

Separate the professional and the personal. You may have formerly entertained your coworkers with tales of Bob's karaoke performance at the local watering hole, but those days are over. Even something as simple as talking about a ball game you'll be attending together may be inappropriate when you are in the presence of other employees.

When you consistently serve up personal anecdotes about your manager, not only will you appear to want people to know that you have an "in" with the boss, but you also risk diminishing the boss's stature in the eyes of the other employees. And when you undercut the person, you weaken the position, an outcome that is not advantageous for your friend or for his or her subordinates, who expect a strong leader.

In general, your mindset should be that when you're on the job you're in a different world, and anything you do or say that brings the personal relationship into play is taboo.

The head of a communication and design firm says, "You have to be hyper-vigilant in your effort to ensure that a friendship doesn't in any way compromise the professionalism of the relationship. I try to safeguard both the business relationship and the friendship by remembering that in the workplace, business comes first."

WHEN YOU'RE THE FRIEND WHO BECOMES THE BOSS . . .

➤ Immediately after your promotion is made public, have a frank conversation with your friend and coworker to set some mutually agreed-on ground rules for your behaviors.

➤ Avoid socializing routinely at lunch or after work. Company-sponsored events, such as the company softball team, are fine.

➤ Manage your friend with an even hand—avoid being too lenient, but don't be too hard on this individual, either.

➤ Focus on department and individual goals to justify your behavior.

➤ Be clear about your expectations from your friend as they pertain to the job.

➤ Explain your preferred management style, and listen to feedback about whether that style is a good fit.

➤ Don't discuss with your friend confidential business matters if you wouldn't tell the entire team.

➤ Never discuss the performance of another team member with your friend who is also your direct report.

Seek out a mentor in another area of the organization. Perhaps because of your real and perceived relationship with your boss/friend, he or she can't provide you with the career advice and opportunities for self-development that you want and need. Any extra time or interest in you shown by the boss may result in negative responses from other coworkers.

It's also possible that you may decide that you don't want to work for your friend for the long term. Regardless of the reason, it may be in your best interest to find someone else in the company who can help you achieve your career goals.

Finding the right mentor isn't always easy. Obviously, you want to align yourself with someone who is generally in favor or, even better, on the way up. The last thing you want is to hitch your wagon to a falling star.

Position yourself so that the person in senior management will want to adopt you as a protégé. Seize opportunities to ask for business-related advice, and target someone who can teach you the basics of doing a good job, share lessons learned from his or her experience, and introduce you to the right people.

If all else fails, ask for a transfer. In some cases, when your friend becomes your boss, immediately changing departments or even jobs may be the answer. "It's not a relationship that everybody can handle," according to Rod Hewitt. "Sometimes, the manager can't make the jump to being the supervisor, and the employee can't accept the friend as a boss. One or other will suffer. Either you won't work well together, or you'll stop being friends." Of course, the chemistry that led to the friendship can contribute to a solid working relationship, and both of you should remember that the friendship was there before the supervisory relationship. The key is leaving work, and the manager/employee relationship, at work and nurturing the friendship away from the office.

THE BOTTOM LINE

- ➤ When your best friend becomes your manager, realize that both of you will be under scrutiny.
- ➤ Working for a manager who is also your friend requires the discipline to separate the personal from the professional while in the office.
- ➤ Identify a mentor from another part of the organization to help coach you through this difficult transition.
- ➤ If all else fails, pursue a transfer or consider a job change.

CHAPTER THIRTY

Dealing with a Bully Boss

*R*emember the playground bully who made you hate recess? Unfortunately, bullies grow up and make their way into the workplace. In many companies, people who love their jobs and are productive contributors dread going to work. Their medicine cabinets are full of antacids and sleep aids. Even highly skilled professionals start to doubt their abilities. If this description sounds all too familiar, you may be suffering at the hands of a bully boss.

BULLY OR DEMANDING MANAGER?

What sets a bully boss apart from the manager who is simply tough and demanding—or perhaps just a grump? The big difference is that bullies make it personal.

You can recognize a bully boss by these behaviors:

➤ Abuses you verbally and nonverbally

➤ Humiliates you in front of others

➤ Doesn't recognize boundaries and intrudes into your personal time (e.g., calls you at 6:00 a.m. when you are on vacation)

➤ Makes you feel like something is wrong with you if you disagree

➤ Never apologizes or admits mistakes

➤ Withholds resources (time, equipment, information, and/or training) to show power or to retaliate

In the schoolyard, bullies tend to pick on smaller or weaker children, often to assert control in an uncertain social environment in which they feel vulnerable. However, adult bullies in positions of authority are often already dominant and in many cases highly successful. Therefore, they are just as likely to pick on a strong subordinate as a weak one, says Dr. Gary Namie, director of the Workplace Bullying and Trauma Institute in Bellingham, Washington. Women are as likely as men to be the aggressors, but women are overwhelmingly the targets.

Unfortunately, this behavior is contagious. Studies show that bullies often spawn mini-bullies in their middle managers or first-line supervisors. Consequently, a bullying culture breeds throughout a department or a company.

WHAT TO DO IF YOU HAVE A BULLY BOSS

While it may seem that you are completely powerless, there are steps you can take to respond to a bully boss.

Avoid becoming a target. Every office bully leaves some people alone. In almost every case they are the people who, from the beginning, refused to be bullied. Stand your ground without flinching and refuse to continue the conversation until the bully settles down. During the interaction, stay calm, look the bully in the eye, deal with the issues, and avoid trying to counter personal attacks.

Don't feed the beast. Some people mistakenly believe that going out of your way to be cooperative, pleasant, and endearing will make the problem go away. Sam Horn, author of *Take the Bully by the Horns: Stop Unethical, Uncooperative, or Unpleasant People from Running and Ruining Your Life*, asserts that attempts to get along with the bully will ultimately backfire, confirming the bully's assessment of your weakness and vulnerability.

Don't count on help from your coworkers. Says Dr. Calvin Morrill, who studies corporate culture at the University of California at Irvine: "Workers become desensitized, tacitly complicit, and don't always act rationally." They're so happy they aren't the target that they will lie low and let you take the heat.

If you choose to report the bully boss, make sure to document incidents thoroughly. If you choose to challenge the bully boss by going to human resources or to the bully's manager, make sure that you carefully document the specifics of each incident, including naming witnesses, advises Jay MacDonald in "Beating a Bullying Boss." Putting it in writing requires the company to follow up or be liable.

Be warned, however, that bullies are often good at "managing up," so their managers may not be aware of the issue and don't want to hear about your problem. Furthermore, most people know that going around your boss is risky, and often the person who reports the bad behavior comes across as a whiner or troublemaker.

If all else fails, cut your losses and leave. You may love your job, but if your discomfort outweighs the rewards, start developing an exit strategy. You don't have to quit on the spot, but commit to finding a better situation. Consider contacting a professional search firm to help you move on.

Unfortunately, in many ways, we live in a *Survivor* world. The aggressive, manipulative tough guy often seems to have the upper hand, even as companies struggle to create productive, supportive communities. Bullies aren't going away, but you can protect yourself by recognizing them and acting decisively to avoid being their victim.

WHAT IF *YOU* ARE THE BULLY? WARNING SIGNS TO ALERT YOU

➤ People look startled or even frightened with you approach them at work.

➤ You ask colleagues, particularly subordinates, to do things for you that you could just as easily do for yourself.

➤ You take your frustrations out on people you see as weak or incompetent.

➤ People hesitate to tell you bad news.

➤ You blame others when things go wrong.

➤ You tend to label people as naysayers, freeloaders, complainers, (according to Susan Annunzio of thebuildnet work.com).

➤ You rarely apologize.

THE BOTTOM LINE

➤ Know the difference between a bully boss and a demanding manager.

➤ Realize that bullies target people they see as weak or vulnerable.

➤ Bullies in positions of power often spawn "mini-bullies" in an organization.

➤ Recognize when you need to cut your losses and leave the situation.

CHAPTER 31

Dealing with Negative Coworkers

*W*e all know these people. You comment that it's a beautiful day, and Jennifer complains about the high pollen count. Bob excitedly tells about last night's win for the home team, and Derek reminds everyone that they will surely choke in the playoffs.

At work, you bring in a new customer or client, and a staff member complains about how much extra work the new account will create. Negativity, whether it's in the workplace or in our personal relationships, can be exhausting, depressing, and often contagious.

UNDERSTANDING NEGATIVITY'S CAUSES AND EFFECTS

Sometimes workplace negativity stems from legitimate causes that need action from management. Author and consultant Susan Heathfield lists such factors as excessive workloads, anxiety about the future, and boredom as reasons for widespread negativity in companies.

In these cases, management has the responsibility to examine company strategy and performance, keep people informed, and provide sufficient and appropriate recognition for good performance.

But what about a particular person who insists on looking at everything from a negative perspective in an otherwise functional office, department, or team? You can recognize these people by the fact that nothing escapes being a target for their complaints. In "How to Cope with Negative Coworkers," Tomiko Cary points out that these people complain about their work, office politics, cafeteria food, building temperature, and other coworkers—not to mention what's going wrong with their personal lives.

If you fall victim to this perpetual assault on your initiative and good humor, here are a few things you and your coworkers can do.

Try to identify the cause of the negative attitude. Negative people often feel alienated from the rest of the group for a variety of reasons. They may suffer from a feeling of inferiority and try to elevate themselves by being the dose of reality that everyone needs. Pointing out why something is doomed to failure or disparaging someone's ideas makes negative people feel more important or unusually knowledgeable. Unlike someone who presents a thoughtful critical evaluation of an issue or raises valid points for discussion, the negative person dismisses out of hand anything and everything as unworkable, substandard, or just plain stupid.

Often these people feel unappreciated and are struggling for attention—even negative recognition. The attitude may stem from either temporary or permanent situations outside the office. Understanding the cause may help you respond appropriately.

On the other hand, negativity does sometimes command attention from others. In their book *The Knowing-Doing Gap*, Jeffrey Pfeffer and Robert L. Sutton acknowledge that negative, hypercritical people in organizations are often perceived by others as smarter. They cite Harvard professor Teresa Amabile's study, entitled "Brilliant but Cruel," which noted that people who read negative book reviews thought that the reviewers were smarter than those whose who wrote complimentary reviews. She concluded that somehow pessimism sounds "profound" while optimism sounds "superficial." So the negative coworker may have experienced a certain level of reinforcement along the way.

If a need for attention is driving the negative behavior, give recognition or responsibility where appropriate. Provide positive feedback to Negative Nell when she does something noteworthy and valuable. Sometimes genuine praise leads to a more affirmative response. Don't allow the person to dismiss your compliment or come back with something disparaging about herself. Be firm in your assertion that the person has done something noteworthy and valuable, and show how it benefits the company or the department.

Furthermore, require the person to take some ownership for activities. If the negative coworker complains about the last office party, put him in charge of the next function (perhaps a small one) or assign the person responsibility for refreshments at the next staff meeting. It's easy to stand on the sidelines and criticize, but when someone owns a project, that person understands the challenges of pleasing everyone.

Point out times when negative expectations didn't materialize. Give the negative person specific examples of other instances in which that individual predicted doom and gloom and things actually turned out fine. "Jennifer, you remember when you insisted that the new receptionist wasn't going to work out? She was just named employee of the month." Or, "Marcus, the new manager you were convinced was going to fire you thinks you are doing a great job."

Too many times, negative comments become habitual because people don't think they will ever be held accountable for their statements. Letting them know that you remember and recognize the inconsistency between their perception and the reality may help them reevaluate their knee-jerk negative reactions.

You can also counter blanket negative statements with examples of positive occurrences that neutralize the general statements. You can offset remarks such as "No one ever recognizes hard work around here" with an example of how Marcus got a nice bonus for his innovative solution to a customer service issue and received a write-up on the company website. However, trying to respond to every negative statement with a positive rejoinder may be a futile effort. Mention a couple of positives, and then either change the subject or find an excuse to disengage. Don't let yourself become a captive audience by spending an inordinate amount of time trying to convince a negative mentality to feel otherwise.

Let the person know how a negative attitude affects you. Times are challenging, and we need to support each other with realistic optimism and reasons to hope. Make sure that the negative coworker understands that his or her toxic attitude is making bad situations worse and interfering with everyone's ability to celebrate victories, however small. Although you should not speak for others, you can make your own feelings apparent, and if other coworkers complain about the negative employee, you might encourage them to share their feelings with the offender rather than simply making that person a topic of office gossip.

IF ALL ELSE FAILS, KEEP YOUR DISTANCE

Let's face it. Someone who has developed a negative attitude over a lifetime probably isn't going to change, regardless of your efforts. If you make a genuine attempt to help your coworker overcome negativism to no avail, then don't let yourself fall under the influence. Avoid asking that person's opinion about something you intend to do or expecting any kind of validation regarding the environment, other employees, or strategic initiatives. Be courteous and friendly, but avoid conversations that may encourage the unwanted behavior.

You and others should make a concerted effort to keep new employees from falling victim to this person's bleak outlook. If you see things affecting the company or the performance of others, consider talking with your manager. If you are the manager, you may need to take action, depending on the severity of the situation.

Negative coworkers can put a damper on everyone's attitude and undermine productivity and camaraderie. Recognizing the symptoms and refusing to let negativism run rampant in your organization will benefit the entire corporate culture and create an atmosphere where people enjoy doing their best.

THE BOTTOM LINE

- ➤ Negativity in the workplace can affect morale and productivity.
- ➤ Realize that a negative attitude has an effect on others.
- ➤ Discerning the cause of someone's negative attitude can help find a way to combat it.
- ➤ Sometimes you simply have to distance yourself from the negative person to avoid the effects on you and your work.

CHAPTER 32

Silence Is Not a Virtue

How to Complain Without Carping

You work hard to prepare a presentation for a key client, but the marketing department is late in providing you with key data you need to complete the report.

Your team is responsible for an important year-end analysis of the company's new product line, and everyone is pulling together and working hard to get the assignment done—except for one team member, who has apparently got more important things to do.

You check out at your hotel only to discover the next day that the front desk clerk charged you twice for your minibar purchases.

*A*ll too often, we must tolerate poor service and lackluster performance. Others make mistakes, and we're the ones who feel the pain. These events often occur when you're stressed and short of time. Do you let it go, or do you find the appropriate person to handle the problem and let it be known that all is not right with the way business is getting done? If you typically let yourself be a victim, the pattern will probably continue. Of course, it takes energy to make a trip to the boss's office or the customer service desk. In addition, if you complain at work, you might fear reprisal or being labeled a troublemaker, but staying silent is a sure way to let a negative pattern continue.

COMPLAINING WITH A PURPOSE

As with criticism, complaints properly given can be constructive. By complaining effectively, without attacking or demeaning another person, you have created a situation where the problem can be solved.

After all, it's always possible that the company or your manager was unaware that the problem even existed.

Of course, in reality you may be confronting a person or a firm that really doesn't care. For example, although they may not be conscious of it, some companies believe that with so many customers out there, losing one won't matter much. Similarly, some firms hold that same attitude toward their employees, and employees tend to treat customers in much the same way that their managers treat them. If that's the case, complaining may not accomplish a great deal.

If you do business with or work for such a firm, you have a choice to make. Will you stop doing business with that company or look for another job? Or are other factors strong enough to make you endure the bad treatment or poor service? We face this dilemma as in our business as well as in our personal lives.

Suppose, for example, that your department head has chosen you to lead a task force and each week one particular colleague shows up without having completed her assignment, wasting everyone's time and slowing progress. It's driving you crazy, but it's also true that when she actually does complete her task, no one can match her creativity and superior insights. Is her talent worth everyone's time and energy spent accommodating her casual attitude toward deadlines? Would speaking with her or her supervisor help solve the problem?

In my own experience, I shop at a supermarket where substandard service is fairly common. Yet it's by far the closest grocery store to where I live, and time is a valuable commodity for me, like it is for most people. So, although my complaints rarely produce more than a perfunctory apology and almost no follow-up, I choose to shop there at least 90 percent of the time because I simply don't want to travel out of my way to pick up something for dinner.

When you complain about a situation, whatever the outcome, at least you know where you (and other colleagues or customers) stand with that person or organization. Then the choice about whether to continue to tolerate the problem is yours.

For the moment, the store's convenience and the well-stocked shelves outweigh the relatively poor service, but I don't feel victimized because I've made the decision to keep shopping there. I'm in control. If I had never complained but then came to terms with the lack of response, I would still be moaning about my unacceptable treatment.

Most companies know that someone who takes the trouble to complain is someone who wants to continue doing business with them. Unhappy customers or clients who don't complain often just go away. So a complaining customer is one who genuinely wants to fix the problem so that the relationship can continue. The same is true in the workplace. You might decide to continue working with the creative woman who is always late on her assignments—if you like your job and enjoy the opportunity created by heading up the task force, you may have little choice. But if you speak with her about it, while it's unlikely she'll change completely, she may change some of the time. If she doesn't, you might talk with your boss about the situation, or you might just decide to endure it for the value she brings to the process. The choice will be yours.

You have the right to complain when you don't get what you have paid for or are entitled to. However, you want to make sure that you do it in such a way that the outcome is as positive as possible for everyone involved. Consider the following guidelines.

Complain to the person who can make a difference. Often we vent to the nearest pair of ears when something displeases us. And all too often, our problem may result from a failure of company policy rather than the actions of the frontline employee.

If you are dealing with an insolent or incompetent coworker, the person may ignore your complaint as long as it's just between the two of you.

Politely, find out the name of the customer service manager or that person's boss. Then contact him or her. My father used to carry a small notepad in his suit pocket. When he encountered poor service, rudeness, or lack of response, he would pull out his little pad and a pen and ask the person: "Now, tell me your name, please." And, while the person looked on, he would carefully write the name down, often verifying the spelling. Amazingly, that small act often changed the demeanor of a discourteous or lackadaisical clerk or manager.

When we need to complain about a situation at work, we are often tempted to talk to colleagues who may agree but who can't change the situation. A manager who routinely announces after lunch on Friday that he needs the team to come in on Saturday morning is a great subject for break room grumbling, but until someone tells the boss or HR manager about the hardship that this behavior causes, things won't get any better.

Be descriptive rather than judgmental. Whenever you give any kind of feedback, describe the situation accurately rather than your interpretation of it. This focus minimizes the emotions that arise when we pass judgment on the incident. In dealing with a vendor at work, for example, you might say something like, "When I asked the sales rep for information about your new product, he replied that I could look it up on the company's website," rather than saying, "When I asked the sales rep for help, he blew me off and gave me a lot of attitude."

In the first instance, the sales rep's manager can deal with the facts of the rep's behavior rather than your interpretation of the way you have been treated.

Avoid getting angry. In many cases, situations that compel us to complain often spark a fair amount of anger. When we become angry, we lose sight of the issue and tend to focus on personalities. You move into a win-lose posture that will probably antagonize the other side and cause the other person to become more defensive or aggressive. Your demeanor becomes contagious, and the situation escalates into a more complex problem that is harder to solve. Think before you speak, and choose your words carefully. Keep your voice soft but firm, and make sure, if you are face-to-face, that your body language doesn't send excessively negative signals.

In many encounters, a little compassion can pay dividends. We don't know what kind of day a person may be having or how the customer before you behaved. Make an attempt to connect with the other person as a human being while keeping focused on the issue.

Suggest a solution. Generally, when we complain, we have a mental picture of how we would like the situation to be. Make sure that you have clearly thought out and precisely presented a solution that would satisfy you. For example, if your online order is late, ask the company to remove the shipping charges. If your particular solution isn't accepted, ask for an alternative solution.

Thank the person who solves the problem. When someone responds positively to your complaints, make sure that you let that person, and others in the organization, know that you appreciate their action. And don't forget to tell your colleagues, if they are aware of the situation and it's appropriate, about the favorable response that you received.

WHEN YOUR COMPLAINTS ARE WELL-RECEIVED

As important as it is to let your dissatisfaction be known when you don't get the cooperation, service, or treatment you deserve and expect, it's equally important to give positive feedback when the opposite situation occurs. You can't assume that people will improve their behaviors if they don't 1) have a clear idea about what constitutes exceptional performance and 2) know precisely when they have met or exceeded your expectations.

When someone solves a problem or, even better, behaves exceptionally to begin with, let that person know. When feasible, tell that person's manager or write a letter to the organization, too. Be diligent about getting what you want, but be sure to recognize when someone meets or exceeds your expectations.

Making sure that you compliment as well as complain sets you apart from the chronic whiner and gives you the credibility that will serve you well in future situations.

Being able to complain without being a complainer benefits us all. Coworkers learn important developmental lessons. Companies keep loyal customers. And we as consumers feel well served and confident that we invested our time, energy, and resources in the right places.

THE BOTTOM LINE

➤ We often avoid complaining because we don't think it will do any good or we fear being labeled a troublemaker.

➤ Refusing to complain encourages negative patterns.

➤ Complain to someone who can make a difference.

➤ Be specific, and avoid getting angry.

➤ Be as generous with compliments as with complaints.

CHAPTER 33

An Apology Is in Order

Repairing the Damage with a Sincere Response

*I*t's unrealistic to think that we can go through life without ever having to apologize for either omissions or commissions of some sort. From the time that we first learned to say "I'm sorry, Mommy. I won't ever do that again," we find ourselves in situations where we have to do damage control. We forgot a lunch appointment. We overlooked a birthday or anniversary. We embarrassed a friend by telling others something he didn't want us to repeat. We snapped at a coworker because we were under stress. We neglected to tell the boss that the meeting had been canceled. And these are just some of the small things for which we might have to apologize.

Most of us find making an apology an unpleasant task at best. First of all, we have to make contact with the person or persons we have offended, upset, or injured, when we'd rather hide out for a while. Second, apologizing usually requires admitting that we were wrong— something most of us don't relish doing. Furthermore, for many of us, apologizing means assuming an inferior position or giving someone else the upper hand. Even worse, if the person to whom we apologize refuses to accept it, we feel rejected and rebuffed.

Without a doubt, apologizing puts us in a vulnerable position. However, a sincere apology handled well, whether in business, in personal relationships, or in an encounter with a stranger, can be a healing, renewing experience, not only for the receiver of the apology but also for the giver.

THE REWARDS OF APOLOGIZING

When you find yourself in a situation that requires an apology, a few guidelines may make your efforts more productive.

Avoid trite, catch-all statements. I usually feel underserved and offended when the apology entails the cliché, "I'm sorry for any inconvenience." We've all heard that from businesses that cause us problems. If people are already angry, this brush-off makes them madder. And the word "any" implies that no one has bothered to consider the specific effect of the mistake or oversight has produced. In fact, this tired old phrase almost creates an element of doubt about the whole thing, as if to say, "You're such a whiner. You probably weren't really inconvenienced at all, but just in case, we're sort of sorry."

Rather than relying on shopworn platitudes, let people know that you really do understand the difficulty that the situation has caused or the hurt and anger that have resulted from your words and actions (or inactions). For example, say, "I'm sorry that I was late in providing you with the information you asked me for. I know that my lack of response caused you to miss your deadline," or, "I apologize that you had to make four calls to track me down. I know you're busy, and I understand how frustrating it is to need to talk to someone who is unavailable." Even though you may not have intentionally caused the problem, at least you let people know that you recognize their dilemma.

Focus on solutions. Making excuses or explaining *why* something happened won't appease most people. And telling people how you will prevent the incident from occurring in the future doesn't do much for the person who is on the receiving end of the mishap. It immediately raises the question, "Why didn't you do that before it happened to me?" When you are responsible for something going wrong, apologize and take responsibility for setting things straight. Whether it's an irate customer, an unhappy supervisor, or a wronged friend, results count. For that reason, finding and implementing solutions add clout to the apologetic words. If the way to resolve the situation is obvious, simply announce what you intend to do, and do it. If, however, the solution is less clear, you may want to present a couple of options and let the other person make the choice. Sometimes, involving people in generating solutions not only starts to rebuild the relationship but also lets them know that you are committed to making things right.

Be sincere. We've all heard celebrities issue faux apologies that deflect the issue and merely focus on the other person's reaction to whatever the offender did. "I'm sorry you are upset." "I regret the way that *you* interpreted my words." This approach sounds like an apology, but it doesn't cause the person to accept responsibility for his or her behavior.

Some people grudgingly apologize when they've run out of all other options. As a result, the apology comes across as a kind of demand to forget it. "Hey, I said I'm sorry. Isn't that enough?" Or their words might say "I'm sorry" while their body language and tone of voice say "I'm only doing this to shut you up!"

Apologizing means genuinely regretting what happened and being dedicated to avoiding any action that would cause the problem again. If you can't send a convincing message that you're sorry in a face-to-face encounter, try putting it in writing (sending flowers may be appropriate in some situations).

End on a positive note. After you've apologized, the conversation may still center on the rift. Make sure that you bring some closure to the situation and reestablish rapport so that you can avoid awkwardness at the next encounter. You can try shifting to a neutral or positive subject before ending the dialogue. "Oh, by the way, Isabel, I hear you've gotten started on the Morrison project. How did the fact-finding meeting go?" Or, "John, How does your son like his new bike?" Turning the conversation in another, less sensitive direction helps normalize the situation and moves both parties forward in the relationship.

Avoid overuse of "I'm sorry." While some of us have trouble apologizing, others seem to apologize too often. People who use the words "I'm sorry" to excess seem to be apologizing all the time and therefore dilute an actual apology when it's necessary. We all know individuals who are habitually "sorry." "I'm sorry. You have the wrong number." "I'm sorry. I must not have made myself clear." "I'm sorry, George. Can we go over that again?" "I'm sorry. I don't have that information. Janice has it." "I'm sorry. I was out when you called."

In these cases, the "I'm sorry" isn't really an apology but rather a conversation smoother. As communication expert and author Deborah Tannen puts it, you're expressing regret without assigning or taking blame. And although taking others' feelings into account is an admirable position, overdoing "I'm sorry" can reflect negatively on your competence and self-assurance.

ACCEPTING AN APOLOGY GRACEFULLY

If you happen to be the one receiving an apology, accept it. A few words may not come close to compensating for the hurt or damage a situation has caused, but refusing to accept an apology diminishes the chances of salvaging the relationship. Even if the apology can't mend the situation, at least you can thank the person for taking the time to talk to you.

In some cases, you may in fact need to share some of the blame. For example, "I should have reminded you that those numbers were critical to the decision process." If such a response isn't appropriate or if the apology is inadequate or insincere, accept the attempt as a step in the right direction and allow the person to save face. Remember that it probably won't be too very long before you find yourself having to issue an apology of your own, and you'll be grateful for a gracious response.

THE BOTTOM LINE

- ➤ Most of us find apologizing to be an unpleasant task because it means admitting we were wrong and because we fear being rebuffed.

- ➤ Apologize with sincerity and explain how you will solve the problem.

- ➤ End an apology on a positive note to smooth the way for future communication.

- ➤ Be receptive when you are on the receiving end of an apology.

- ➤ A sincere, well-handled apology, whether in business, in personal relationships, or in an encounter with a stranger, can be a healing, renewing experience for the receiver and for the giver.

- ➤ Being gracious when accepting someone's apology goes a long way toward repairing the relationship.

CHAPTER 34

Delivering Unwelcome Information Without Damaging Relationships

Your throat feels tight and your palms are sweating. You need to take a few breaths in a paper bag. Are you waiting to begin a huge presentation to snag your competition's biggest client? Are you tuning up to sing the national anthem at the World Series? Actually, you are preparing for a meeting with an employee to whom you must deliver unwelcome information about performance, a raise, or a promotion that isn't going to happen, or worse, about an impending layoff.

*M*ore than 2,500 years ago, Socrates noted that "none love the messenger who brings bad news." Perhaps no situation taxes our ability to be courteous and clear at the same time as when we are delivering information that our audience doesn't want to hear. However, as our careers ascend and responsibilities increase, one of the realities of power is the need to deliver messages that people don't want to hear. One CFO remarked that about 80 percent of her communication involves conveying unwelcome messages.

Even in relationships built on excellent communication, communicating when one or both parties are under stress increases the opportunities for communication breakdown. Whether in the workplace, at home, or in social situations, being able to deliver unwelcome information without damaging or destroying a relationship can be a huge asset both personally and professionally.

Most of us find the process intimidating either because we fear the recipient's reaction, we don't handle conflict effectively, or we don't want to come across as a bully. When we do attempt to deliver the news, we dance around the issue or sugarcoat it to the point that the real message may be lost on the recipient.

Although the process will never be easy or enjoyable, having a strategy for delivering bad news can help the process go more smoothly. Furthermore, most of the unwelcome information we deliver involves people with whom we interact regularly and who are often professional friends. With a thoughtful approach, you have a much better chance of keeping the relationship intact and positive.

PLANNING FOR SUCCESS

An MBA student told me about a manager at a company where he worked who hated to deliver unwelcome information. A situation arose in which he had to tell a member of the department that he was terminating her employment, so he called her into his office at the end of the day, presumably to deliver the bad news. The next morning, she showed up for work, as usual. He had been so vague in his meeting with her that she had no idea her manager had fired her.

The fact that we aren't crazy about delivering unwelcome information makes us reluctant to think about how we should deliver the message. Consequently, we often put it off until the last minute and then just blurt out whatever comes to mind. The result is often disjointed, unorganized, and unpleasant for both parties. At one extreme, there's the blunt, callous delivery: "Sorry. That's not gonna happen!" At the other end of the spectrum is the mealy-mouthed, overly passive, blame-other-people-or-circumstances approach: "If it were up to me, I'd give you another chance, but the boss is on a tear about absenteeism."

Then we have the passive-aggressive approach, where someone says "yes" and does "no." This person never conveys the unwelcome information clearly and instead waits for the issue to evaporate as a result of his or her inaction.

Delivering bad news takes special thought and planning. In many cases, the person whose request you have to refuse or who will receive some other kind of unwelcome information is someone with whom you have an ongoing relationship. For that reason, you want to deliver the message in a way that inflicts as little damage as possible to the relationship.

The following suggestions, tailored to individual situations, may help you the next time you have to deliver unwelcome news.

Clarify your objectives. Be realistic about what to expect from your audience. The best-case scenario will be that the receiver of the news will both understand and accept what you have to say. Don't expect the person to like it or to be happy. That reaction would come from good news.

In addition, you want to minimize the potential bad feelings toward you and your company, and you want to send a message of fairness. As you plan your communication, keep your objectives in mind.

Choose the right time and place. Know that your message isn't going to make someone's day, so the setting in which you deliver the bad news is important. If at all feasible, deliver the message in person. You need all the tools in your communication tool kit to handle sensitive and perhaps emotional situations. e-mail and even the telephone don't deliver the "bandwidth" to allow you to do your best.

Similarly, consider the other person's immediate circumstances. If that person is already having a stressful day, hold off on having the conversation until stress levels decrease. Unless your schedule won't permit a delay, don't let your bit of bad news be the proverbial straw that broke the camel's back.

Break the news in private. Don't add embarrassment to disappointment. Even if the situation seems trivial to you, you don't know where it lies on the other person's list of priorities. Be sensitive to the other person's feelings and status, and don't make public an issue that can be kept private.

Plan your setup. If you want to get anywhere with a hostile audience, consider introducing your conversation with something other than the bad news, except of course in cases of a real tragedy or where you know the person so well and the trust level is such that you don't need any preamble. Generally speaking, however, you should introduce the conversation in a way that opens the door for the dialogue that you have planned. Some authorities on the subject suggest a bad news sandwich, in which you enclose the bad news with a positive message on either end. Although I agree that ending with a goodwill builder makes good sense, I believe that most people are smart enough to recognize a "positive" comment that leads to the big "but . . ."

Leading into your unwelcome message with a couple of neutral statements may be a better choice. For example, Mario may say to his employee: "Bob, you asked me to check the schedule and see if you could take Friday off without inconveniencing another team member or stalling a project. I checked with Kirk and Keisha, and they really need you to help with compiling the market test results that will come in on Thursday."

Mario has let Bob know that he understands his request and made an attempt to grant it. However, Mario fell short by not clearly stating his decision. Mario should have concluded by adding, "For that reason, I can't grant your request to take Friday off because we really need your expertise on this project." Make sure that you leave no doubt when you actually break bad news.

On the other hand, if the news is going to be devastating, you may simply want to say, "I have some bad news," and then get to the point quickly and clearly. Don't keep the person in suspense.

Provide explanations if appropriate. From our earliest years, we react negatively when someone delivers an unpleasant message with either no explanation or with "That's just the way it is" as a reason. Knowing why something is "the way it is" can take some of the sting out of the disappointment. In the previous example, Bob may have been less disappointed or annoyed if his manager Mario had explained that Bob couldn't have the day off because the market test results were supposed to have been available three days earlier, and now the turnaround time has become much tighter.

Acknowledge changes in circumstances that may have governed the decision. If a situation has changed from what was originally understood, acknowledge that fact. "Ken, I know we thought that Makayla from Operations was going to be able to help us on this project, but she had emergency surgery yesterday morning." This information is important because it impacts your credibility. It validates your reasons for making a specific decision. We are all familiar with those companies that have for years insisted that they would never lay off any employees. But when the day comes that they have to change their policy, these firms often develop historical amnesia when communicating with their workforce.

Review the alternatives considered. If you tried to avoid the situation, say so, and present some alternatives to the person receiving the bad news. People are usually more willing to accept circumstances if they understand the cause behind them. Giving reasons and answering some questions can take some of the sting out of the other person's disappointment or frustration.

Furthermore, letting people know that you have considered alternatives before coming back with the unwelcome answer or solution sends a powerful message that you haven't made your decision frivolously. For example, if you are asking members of your staff to work late for the next two weeks to meet a project deadline, they will be more responsive if you also explain that you tried hard to secure a later due date and that you requested a temp for the department but management turned down your request.

Demonstrate empathy and respond appropriately. Let people know what their sacrifice will mean in the bigger picture. Help them understand that you recognize the personal inconvenience they are experiencing and that you value their contribution. Even if a particular task is part of the job description, let people know that you have a deep sense of appreciation for what they are doing and that you value them as people as well as employees. Salaries are only part of the reward people seek for working in a particular position.

Don't expect things to improve immediately. As with any communication, you should have a desired outcome in mind, and when you are delivering unwelcome information, about the best you can hope for is acceptance and understanding. After all, if people were going to be happy about it, the news wouldn't qualify as bad. Know that the recipient of bad news may feel lousy at the moment, so avoid the temptation to say, "I understand how you feel," because you don't. Even if you have had similar experiences, you can't know exactly what another person's feelings are.

Create goodwill. Remember that most of the time we find ourselves having to deliver unwelcome information, it is going to involve people we interact with regularly, and it's important to strive to maintain a good relationship in spite of the bad news. You can accomplish this goal by shifting the focus from the unpleasant situation to something more positive, either as compensation or as a goodwill gesture. Let's return to the earlier example of Mario, the manager, and Bob, his employee. Mario may end the conversation by reassuring Bob that he will arrange for some extra time off for him once the project gets completed. Or he may order pizza on the Friday everyone is under the gun. Try to be creative about how you move others' focus off the unwelcome situation and increase their willingness to move past it.

Stand firm, but be compassionate. When you have to say "no," consider these factors: Is your answer definitive under any and all circumstances, or are there conditions under which you would change your mind? Can you give a "not at this time" answer and agree to revisit the situation later?

Sometimes, when you have to say "no" or deliver any other unwelcome news, your audience may get angry and want to argue. Refuse to lose your cool, but know that you don't have to take abuse, either. Calmly and quietly state that you don't intend to continue the conversation under those circumstances. Tell the other person that you will be glad to resume the discussion when he or she can regain composure.

In some cases, you may have to state your message more than once to get through to the person who has thrown up all kinds of resistance and still objects to the decision. For example, you may not be able to convince an employee that her best friend's baby shower isn't as critical as a huge presentation to the company's biggest client. Reiterate your reasons, if appropriate, and acknowledge the person's frustration and disappointment, but stick to your message.

Along with standing your ground, it's also important not to come across as insensitive. However, in an effort to show concern, don't resort to hackneyed expressions and platitudes such as "Things will look better in the morning" or "Every cloud has a silver lining." Not only are they ineffective, but you come across as shallow and insincere. Saying something simple such as "I know that you are disappointed, and I wish the situation were different" lets people know you care about their feelings. Your genuine and straightforward demeanor will go a long way toward helping people accept the situation.

WHEN YOU'RE THE RECIPIENT OF BAD NEWS. . . . . .

➤ Listen to the entire message before reacting.

➤ Be open about how you're currently feeling so that the sender will understand if you can't help becoming emotional.

➤ At the same time, avoid irrational emotional outbursts.

➤ Paraphrase what you heard.

➤ Acknowledge valid points.

➤ Ask for specific examples. Don't accept vague generalities such as "You have a bad attitude."

➤ If the unwelcome information is about your behavior, don't counterattack with your own observations about the sender. ("You're late as often as I am.")

➤ If necessary, ask for time to process the information.

➤ Clarify next steps.

Breaking bad news is never easy or pleasant, but few situations give you an opportunity to show your integrity and grace. Learning to deliver unwelcome information with honesty, courtesy, and respect for the person receiving the bad news can contribute to stronger relationships in the long term.

THE BOTTOM LINE

➤ Delivering bad news takes special thought and planning. When it's feasible, offer an explanation and explain alternatives that you considered.

➤ Always strive to end an unwelcome message with neutral or positive communication to smooth the way for future communication.

➤ Stick to your message, but show sensitivity by acknowledging the person's frustration and disappointment.

➤ Being able to deliver unwelcome information without damaging or destroying the relationship can be a huge asset both personally and professionally.

CHAPTER 35

Confronting with Courtesy

Preserving Relationships While Resolving Differences

*C*onfrontation and conflict are natural phenomena that grow out of many kinds of competitive endeavors, and certainly a highly charged business environment full of intelligent, creative people provides fertile ground for honest disagreement. Confrontation and conflict are among the forces that, when properly managed, accelerate a company's growth and performance. However, issues such as limited resources, contradictory interpretations of business strategies or plans, and differing methods to achieve goals all provide abundant opportunities for people to become proprietary, frustrated, and even confrontational and combative.

Few people actually enjoy disagreement, whether it occurs with a recalcitrant colleague, an offended friend, an angry boss, or an unhappy customer. Although some people seem to thrive on adversarial situations, most of us, when faced with conflict, run for cover, give in immediately, jump to a no-win compromise, or generally handle it poorly.

Furthermore, conflict presents the potential for undesirable long-term consequences. If we typically win all of our disputes, we develop a reputation as a bully. If we give in too easily, we're viewed as wimpy. If we just avoid the issue, nothing gets resolved or the problem morphs into something worse.

LEVELS AND SOURCES OF CONFLICT

Conflict appears in the workplace at various levels. Peg Pickering, author of *How to Manage Conflict: Turn All Conflicts into Win-Win Outcomes*, refers to three stages of conflict that range from everyday irritations, to more serious challenges with higher consequences, to harmful situations where the desire to win is surpassed by the desire to punish. What stage of conflict we encounter depends on a variety of factors: the importance of the issue, pride and ego, values, personalities, and even our skill (or lack thereof) at handling disagreements and confrontations.

Conflict in the workplace results from multiple causes. It can grow out of scarcity of resources. For example, two people need one available copier for a big job, or the secretarial pool has gotten too shallow for everyone's project, or, on a more personal level, there is just one available promotion that two people are vying for. Conflict may also arise out of differing values: Some people in an organization may take great pleasure in making themselves look good—at other people's expense.

Conflict often grows out of incorrect assumptions or incomplete or bad information. For example, you get angry because when Pat needs to talk to you, she always has her administrative assistant get you on the phone and put you on hold. You assume that in placing phone calls this way, she considers her time more valuable than yours.

Interestingly, conflict also grows out of open communication. The more everyone feels comfortable speaking freely, the more likely disagreements will arise. In these situations, we should remember that confrontations are neither good nor bad. It's all in how they are handled. Handled poorly, conflicts in the workplace will shut down the open flow of communication, negatively affecting trust, productivity, and morale.

AVOIDING THE HIGH COST OF UNRESOLVED CONFLICT

Left unresolved, conflict can paralyze relationships. At work, when team members or departments stop working together it leads to duplication of effort and resources, and important results are diminished, blocked, or altered.

In many cases, benefits can arise from the successful collaboration and resolution of opposing views, in the form of better problem solving, unconstrained creativity, and greater organizational unity. The challenge, then, is how to handle conflict in a way that can be tough on the issues and soft on the people. Here are some generally accepted suggestions.

Deal with the issue quickly. When I was a child, my mother taught me not to go to bed angry. The old adage, "Don't let the sun go down on your anger," makes a similar point: When we let unpleasant situations fester, we may end up with a problem that started out as trivial but has grown more intense as we stewed over it.

Resolving conflicts quickly, however, doesn't mean that you should blurt out your displeasure or disagreement the moment you perceive the disturbance. Reflect on the situation long enough to plan how you want to position your remarks and decide when and where you want to discuss the issue. Confrontations in front of an audience are rarely successful. Few situations put people on the defensive faster than being embarrassed publicly.

If the situation is a mild disagreement that you can settle immediately, such as a differing view in a problem-solving meeting, make sure that you approach the subject in a nonthreatening way that preserves the dignity and reputation of the other person. You might say something like, "I have a slightly different perspective on this issue that I'd like to share with you."

The way you introduce your position can make a world of difference. I was once in a meeting where a junior executive brought up a point that he obviously thought was a great concept. The reaction he received was: "You're about two years too late with that idea!" He didn't say another word for the rest of the discussion, and the possibilities for exploring variations of his suggestion went by the wayside.

Ask questions to gain perspective. Information and understanding are great deterrents to destructive conflict. The more you know about the person's reasons for behaving a certain way, the better chance you both have of resolving things to mutual satisfaction. Furthermore, getting the straight story, if possible, keeps you from assigning motives to someone's behavior. Taking it upon yourself to determine why someone behaved in a particular way is usually a quick way to escalate anger.

If you're curious about the reason for someone's behavior, by all means ask—but in a nonthreatening way. One way to avoid being adversarial in your questioning is to avoid questions that begin with "why." In a situation where no conflict is present, employing "why" questions can be very illuminating. But when you add a touch of conflict to the issue, questions that begin with "why" can put people on the defensive immediately.

Finding out the underlying reasons for observable behavior can also help you in resolving the conflict. Perhaps Allan became agitated and irritable when you asked him how the Marston deal was progressing. His response might be something like, "You're always checking up on me like I can't handle myself in a sales situation." The real problem might lie in the fact that Allan has just gotten word that one of his current customers has reduced its orders for this quarter, and he is looking at a poor quarterly performance if he can't close the Marston deal. He's already putting pressure on himself; the added pressure that he is now feeling from you, either real or imagined, is creating a stressful situation, and he's reacting accordingly.

The more you can find out about both the position that someone takes and the underlying reason for that position, the better your chances for bringing the situation to a positive end for everyone.

In an interesting conflict-resolution exercise, two people are charged with negotiating for possession of a particular fruit (usually an orange or a grapefruit) that, in the fictional scenario, has amazing properties to cure a variety of diseases. At first, things look as though it is an all-or-nothing situation; one or the other must end up in the dominant position. However, as the two sides talk and reveal their reasons for wanting the fruit, they discover that one needs the juice and the other the rind. So, in actuality, no conflict exists.

Obviously, getting to this kind of win-win outcome requires a fairly high level of trust, which is difficult to build instantly once you find yourself in conflict with another person. If you have a reputation for treating people courteously and fairly and valuing them as individuals, when conflicts occur, you will have a much better chance of getting through them unscathed.

Discuss only the here and now. Often when we get into an argument with another person, all the problems we have ever had with that person come surging back into our minds. In some cases, the behaviors that prompted the current conflict have caused conflicts in the past. However, when addressing a conflict, it's important to focus the discussion only on the issue that created the current conflict. For example, say you are dealing with a coworker who was late for a meeting with an important customer. Worse, your colleague had information that kept the meeting from starting on time, and this latest event wasn't the first time you and others had suffered inconvenience and frustration because of this person's tardiness. Regardless of the history, you should focus on the current situation and get the person to concentrate on this particular circumstance and why his or her behavior caused a problem. If you need to have a talk about habitual lateness, do it separately.

Don't overreact; respond appropriately to the situation. Often, in our frustration and anger, we let our own emotions escalate to a fever pitch before we actually engage the other person or group. If you react to coffee-stirrer sticks and used sweetener packets left on the break room counter at the same level that you respond to discovering that the CFO has embezzled the pension fund, then your credibility starts to suffer and you lose the perspective necessary for resolving issues effectively.

Even if the situation is serious, assess the relationship and decide how much anger or energy it will bear. You may have to back off a bit because of the consequences that might result if you reveal the full extent of your feelings.

In any case, be sure to maintain a courteous demeanor with restrained body language during the discussion or disagreement. Remember that you want the relationship to survive this specific situation. You should be able to walk away from a conflict without regrets.

Know also that some people use explosive anger to intimidate others and create a protective wall around them. If you are in conflict with someone who deploys this tactic, call them on their behavior. Say, very calmly, that you will be happy to discuss the matter when they have control of their emotions.

Focus on solutions, not on blame. Conflict often occurs when someone has made a mistake that has negative effects on others, perhaps even an entire organization. The natural tendency is to find a scapegoat and dump all our frustrations on the offender. We may be hurt, or angry, or discouraged by the situation, and frankly, dwelling on the negative is easier than picking up and starting over.

In a great scene from the movie *Apollo 13*, when the flight controller (played by Ed Harris) realizes that the mission has failed and the astronauts' lives are in extreme danger, he says, "Let's work the problem, people." Rather than trying to find out who did what and begin a finger-pointing ritual that wastes precious minutes, the team shifts its focus immediately to finding a way to overcome incredible obstacles and avert doom.

If we can adopt the same attitude when issues arise in our own workplaces, we will not only avoid the backbiting and blaming, but we will also unleash a new level of creativity that finds better answers to challenging situations and ultimately benefits both individuals and organizations.

Preempt the conflict if possible. Although finding ways to resolve conflict is critical, whenever possible, work to keep conflicts from occurring. Assumptions often lead to discord, and if you can replace assumptions with certainty, you can avoid expending energy in resolving disputes.

One way to bypass conflict is to formulate clear agreements up front. Use the journalists' *who, what,* and *when* tenets, along with answering the questions "What if?" and "What's next?" Having answers to these vital questions and verifying that all parties approve the answers can prevent later disagreements about expectations and responsibilities. Let's say that Kendra and Judy decide to give a baby shower for their coworker Martine, who is going on maternity leave next month. The shower will be at the office in the employee lounge in two weeks. While on lunch break with Colleen, Kendra spies some great decorations for a baby shower, including plates, napkins, and paper tablecloths. Colleen encourages her to buy them.

Together, they return to the office and proudly show Judy the purchase, at which time Judy reacts negatively and angrily at being left out of the shower planning activities. The argument quickly escalates.

How could Kendra and Judy have avoided this conflict? What agreements could they have formulated about the baby shower that would have kept a pleasant event from turning sour? Certainly, they needed to answer questions about roles and responsibilities. What would they decide together, what would they do jointly, and what parts of the event would each individual handle?

Get over it and move on. As adults, most of us realize that we're going to be wrong from time to time, and we learned long ago that we aren't always going to get our way. Similarly, people are going to make mistakes that cause us to suffer consequences—and we will, conversely, do the same. If we handle our disagreements in a courteous, nonthreatening manner, without fixing blame, we may find that the outcomes are surprisingly positive and beneficial and that relationships thrive in a stimulating, accepting, and responsive atmosphere.

THE BOTTOM LINE

➤ Most of us, when faced with conflict, run for cover, give in immediately, jump to a no-win compromise, or generally handle it poorly.

➤ Often, benefits arise from the successful collaboration and resolution of opposing views.

➤ Whenever possible, resolve a disagreement quickly.

➤ Confrontation and conflict are natural phenomena that grow out of many kinds of competitive endeavors, and certainly a highly charged business environment provides fertile ground for honest disagreement.

➤ Replacing assumptions with clear and accurate information is a major step toward resolving conflict.

➤ Focus on finding solutions rather than on assigning blame.

➤ Preempt conflict by formulating clear agreements.

➤ The challenge, in the end, is handling conflict in a way that we can be tough on the issues and soft on the people.

CHAPTER 36

When the Worst Happens

Dealing with Tragedy, Illness, and Death

*N*o one escapes the pain of loss and sorrow. Death is as natural as birth for all living things, yet we tend to deny its reality until circumstances bring it home to us in all its fury. Most of us who haven't yet experienced its chilling, debilitating force have known others who have had to suffer their own personal agonies and loss. When it happens, coworkers, neighbors, clients, and friends have to deal with the unimaginable, and often unfamiliar, and want to offer comfort, but struggle to determine what our behavior should be.

Often, even though we may want to reach out to the grieving person or family, the circumstances make us feel uncomfortable and disconcerted—particularly if our relationship is more professional than personal. We simply don't know how to respond or behave in the face of overwhelming private crises.

My own personal nightmare began on a warm spring evening when, just home from a workout and a quick stop at the grocery store, I received a phone call telling me that my nineteen-year-old daughter, while participating in a sorority walk-a-thon at college in another state, had been hit by a motorist and killed instantly. Because she was one of five girls who lost their lives in this tragedy, along with several others who were severely injured, the story made regional and even national media. For this reason, many of my friends and acquaintances learned the terrible news almost as soon as I did.

Before I could even begin to comprehend the horror of what had happened, my home was flooded with friends, neighbors, professional associates, schoolmates of my two daughters, and even the local TV stations. During the next few awful days, I learned a great deal about how important human support can be, and how we all wrestle with the best way to provide the solace and comfort that we want to offer.

DEALING WITH ANOTHER'S GRIEF

Through my own experience and in talking to others who have lost loved ones, faced debilitating illnesses, or dealt with the effects of horrendous accidents, I have discovered some common threads in creating an appropriate and even-handed response. They may help you when you need to express concern and sympathy.

Keep your message simple and compassionate. "I'm so sorry" carries tremendous weight. If you can't think of anything else to say, leave it at that. Or perhaps you might admit your feelings of inadequacy with a statement such as "I wish I could say something of comfort, but words fail me at a time like this." A grieving person will be more responsive to a simple, caring message than a flowery declaration that sounds like a sympathy card.

Be a patient and attentive listener. If you have never experienced the loss of someone very close to you, you may find the bereaved person's behavior odd, and you may feel uncomfortable. You need to remember that when people experience tragedy, their world has stopped. They can't think or focus on anything else. Over the days and weeks, they may seem to be obsessed with their loss, and our natural tendency is to try to help them snap out of it. However, the need to talk and remember the lost or injured loved one is an important part of the healing process. You can be a great source of support to your friend or colleague by being a patient and attentive listener.

Be willing to share memories with the bereaved. We often feel ill at ease talking about the deceased, but remembering events, sharing stories, even humorous ones, can be a great healer. If you didn't know the person who died, ask questions. Most people value keeping the memory of their loved one alive. If the person doesn't want to talk, you will know very quickly and can move to another topic.

I was reminded recently of this need to remember while traveling to another city to meet with a coaching client. I arrived early and found myself in the waiting room of the company, near the receptionist's station. Just making small talk, I asked the receptionist, "How are you today?" She immediately began to tell me, a stranger, that it was the one-year anniversary of her husband's death. For about ten minutes she talked about him, their life together, and how much she missed him. I said almost nothing, but she obviously needed to tell someone about this important day in her life.

Look for ways to be helpful. Too often people offer the generic "If there's anything I can do . . ." Most of the time this cliché isn't taken seriously, or isn't specific enough to help the distraught person. Take the initiative to think about what you can do, and do it. I will never forget the friend who went to the store and bought facial tissue and placed a box in every room of my home. Many years later, her practical and extremely thoughtful act of kindness remains in my mind.

Sometimes, the best ways to help out can be mundane, from picking up cleaning, buying a few groceries, or preparing a meal. If it's a close friend or family member, staying overnight with the family can be an immense source of support. In the case of a death, remember also that the opportunity for the most valued assistance often presents itself in the days after the funeral, when relatives have returned home and friends have gone back to the routine of their own lives.

Don't forget the children in a family. Pay special attention to younger members of a family at the funeral and in the coming days and weeks. We tend to turn our attention to the adults in a tragic situation and forget that children are hurt, confused, and in need of attention that their parents may not be able to give them at the time.

If the deceased is one of the children in the family, remember that siblings feel all sorts of complex feelings, from anger to guilt to denial. At times their behavior can seem bizarre or inappropriate, but remember that they are in uncharted territory, and too often they get lost in the bustle of necessary activity.

Provide reassurance. Many times death comes after a long illness with an extended hospital stay. You may provide a great service by reassuring the bereaved that he or she did everything possible, that the medical care was high quality, and offering any other comforting responses that you know to be true.

People may second-guess their behavior and torment themselves with "if only" and "why didn't I . . ." kinds of thoughts. Help them to understand that no relationship is perfect, and none ends without some regrets.

WHAT NOT TO DO

Sometimes people unintentionally do or say things that cause additional distress or may even be detrimental to someone's ability to deal with the event. Although we can't be 100 percent certain that our actions will have the effect that we intend, here are some pitfalls to avoid, which will increase your chances of handling the situation effectively.

Don't avoid the bereaved. Many times we refrain from being around someone in the throes of a tragic event because we don't know what to say. Discomfort is inevitable, but such a time is an occasion to put your own feelings aside. Your presence can bring comfort even if you don't say much.

Don't offer platitudes. If you're not sure what to say, just stick to something simple, such as "I'm sorry." Above all, remember that this is not the time to drag out clichés such as "Time heals all wounds," or "He's in a better place."

Don't try to explain why things happen. Our deep-seated desire for answers when the unexplainable happens pushes us to grope for the reasons behind death and tragedy. We don't want to admit that we humans are frail and vulnerable and that random events transpire that cause injury and death. However, in our zeal to provide answers, we may raise doubts and questions in the minds of the bereaved that cause more harm than good.

Don't assume your beliefs will be shared or accepted. Unless you are completely familiar with that person's spiritual point of view and share those belief systems, avoid any pronouncements based on your own theology. People come to terms with death or illness according to their own beliefs, and advancing your own ideas about life and death from a faith-based perspective can actually be troubling and unsettling rather than comforting.

Don't judge the behavior of the grieving person. Remember that people will express grief in different ways. Some talk incessantly about the departed, while others keep things to themselves. In the days following a loss, some people maintain a deceased person's room just as it was on the last day of life, while others remove every vestige of reminders that the person lived there. Follow their lead in your response. Allow them to express as much grief as they are feeling and are willing to share. Let them express their emotions and their feelings freely. Resist the temptation to say "Don't cry."

If someone's grieving behavior seems strange or inappropriate to you, suspend your judgment and avoid inserting your own response into that person's behavior. Grief is highly personal, and people deal with pain in vastly different ways. When my daughter died, I welcomed the comfort of friends, acquaintances, professional associates, and even strangers who were parents of my children's friends. Conversely, when a neighbor's husband died suddenly, she and her children parked cars at both ends of their circular drive for several days, as a message to everyone that they needed time alone.

People cope in ways that seem best to them. If, however, you suspect that a particular behavior may be harmful to the grieving person or to others, contact someone qualified to help in such situations. Do not try to handle it yourself.

Don't expect your responses to be perfect. None of us has the answers to life's most perplexing questions. In trying to provide solace, you may say things that seem to aggravate rather than comfort. You're not a trained grief counselor, and no one expects you to know all the right things to say. But you can give something that professionals may be unable to provide—sincerity, caring, and your commitment to your relationship with the grieving friend, neighbor, or colleague.

THE MOST VALUABLE RESPONSE

Of all the things you might say or do to help someone through a period of grief, your presence is the most precious. If your intent is pure, your gestures will be understood and appreciated, even when they seem inadequate to you. The more we can communicate support and understanding through words and acts of kindness, the more we facilitate the journey of life for our fellow travelers—and for ourselves.

THE BOTTOM LINE

➤ Even when we want to respond to the grief of coworkers, neighbors, clients, and friends and offer some kind of comfort, we often struggle with what our behavior should be.

➤ It's natural to feel uncomfortable and disconcerted when trying to provide comfort to someone with whom our relationship is more professional than personal.

➤ If you're not sure what to say, keep it simple and just say "I'm sorry." Above all, avoid clichés and platitudes.

➤ Recognize that people grieve in different ways.

➤ Look for practical ways to help.

➤ Don't expect your response to always be perfect.

CHAPTER 37

Putting It All Together

Creating and Maintaining Your Personal Brand

*N*ike has one. Coca-Cola has one. Apple has one. Certain words and images come to mind when we think of those companies. These companies have a distinctive brand, and that brand translates to significant brand equity—the value that comes from public perception of a company's value that goes beyond the actual worth of the product or service. Similarly, public perception exists regarding people. Celebrities hire professionals to manage the public's perception, in short to manage their personal brand. We've learned our lessons from the companies and famous people—a personal brand is critical in establishing you as a trustworthy, credible, capable colleague. Your personal brand is the total package that presents you to the world, both a first impression and an ongoing, acquired persona. The message that your brand sends needs to be consistent with your abilities, your values, your character, and your general personality style. As Suzanne Bates says in her article on "The Science of Influence: The Three Dimensions of Executive Presence," people come to have expectations about you based on your image, mannerisms, and interpersonal behavior, and a difference in your brand and their expectations can cause people to "judge you as ineffective" or even inauthentic.

The elements of your personal brand are already out there—your field of interests, the schools you attended, the places you have lived, the associations to which you belong, your favorite places to eat and vacation, the sports teams that you support, your family ties—the list goes on and on. Even if you aren't intentionally posting information about yourself online, your buying habits and any location services on your devices are creating an ongoing narrative about you. So, you need to take control of establishing and managing the way you want others to perceive you, or they will do it on their own. And the results may not be what you want.

Establishing and maintaining a strong, positive personal brand requires a deliberate, consistent, and insightful approach that provides opportunities for continued growth.

RECOGNIZING WHAT MAKES YOU UNIQUE

Throughout history, the command of "know thyself" has been a hallmark of positioning human beings for success, so it's not surprising that a significant level of self-awareness is critical to building your personal brand. What are your strengths? What words would people use to describe you? In school, what did you do especially well? You could have some significant talent or athletic ability. You could be known for being a quick study—catching on quickly to ideas or instructions. Are you the person who is always willing to lend a hand when someone needs help? Are you the person who is always calm in a crisis or who always seems to have an innovative solution to a problem?

Take stock of your physical attributes and decide if you want to change anything. Are you wearing clothes and colors that flatter your particular body type? Do you need to improve your fitness? Based on your goals, should you learn a skill, such as being a good presenter, or a sport—for example, golf? What can you do to enhance the image you want to convey?

Make sure that the way you want to come across to others is consistent with your core beliefs and values. Otherwise, the brand that you create will be inauthentic and you will inadvertently present yourself as phony or superficial.

Consider taking a personality or skills assessment to discover the particular strengths and challenges of your natural style. Although we can't really change personality, we can learn to flex or modify our personal style to interact effectively with others. You have to know yourself well to understand how you may share attributes or differ from other people. Being aware of how others differ from you can make a huge difference in how you are able to connect with them.

IDENTIFYING STRATEGIES FOR SUCCESS

Much of developing your brand revolves around understanding others and recognizing the specific characteristics of your environment. Learning how to interact with your surroundings will create a positive response to you in the ways that you want to occur.

Become knowledgeable about the corporate culture where you work.

Organizational savvy is more than simply knowing how to play office politics. It's understanding the unspoken rules and assumptions that are much more critical in your awareness of how your company works than simply being able to recite the mission statement.

If your company's culture were a person, how would you describe it? Is this "person" young, energetic, and risk taking? Warm, friendly, and inclusive? Stodgy, rigid, and retaliatory? Experiencing a middle-aged crisis? Be conscious of what your organization rewards and what it punishes. What is the level of collaboration versus individual performance? Knowing these important differentiators will help you understand how to negotiate agreements, propose new ideas, and handle conflict.

Build trust-based relationships with decision makers you can learn from and who will help you in your development. Building strong relationships is key to success throughout your career, and you should make relationship building a priority in general. However, it is particularly important to develop relationships with those who can give you objective and useful advice or who can advocate for you. We hear a great deal about the importance of having a mentor—usually someone with experience who can share the rewards of a successful career with you and someone who most likely has a strong personal brand. If you develop the kind of relationship that enables open discussion, you can learn much about how you come across to others.

Perhaps even more important is the contribution that an advocate can make in your success. An advocate can promote you in many ways and often can get you in front of people who can make important decisions regarding your career. Keep in mind, however, that an advocate also expects you and your performance to make him or her look good and to validate the advocacy.

Develop an elevator speech that connects with others. We all hear about the importance of an elevator speech—that pithy introduction that makes people want to know more about you and what you and your company do. But all too often, elevator pitches are awkward mini-resumes that just present a list of facts about the person. Develop an opener that speaks to the needs of the audience and how you can meet those needs. Your statements should affirm the audience as well. Chris Westfall, author of *The New Elevator Pitch,* asserts that your speech should demonstrate knowledge of the audience and the subject matter and that you should deliver it with energy and conviction. Craig Harrison of Expressions of Excellence provides some great examples of compelling elevator speeches, for example. Alice Anderson, an attorney who specializes in nonprofit clients, refers to "saving people who are saving the world" in her elevator speech.

DEMONSTRATING YOUR BRAND CONSISTENTLY

You can't turn your brand on and off like a light switch. Even though the initial impression that you make is fundamental to establishing a perception, you must continue to manage your brand and others' perception of you through your consistent and authentic behavior. Don't make the mistake of thinking that your brand is an artificial overlay that you haul out when you want to look good to someone. Your brand has to come from the core of who you are—your belief system, your values, and the attitudes that emerge from those established principles.

Find the right balance of openness with others so that they know who you are and how to deal with you. The more open you are with other people, the more they will be willing, in most cases, to self-reveal. Through this mutual sharing, you lay the foundation for building trust. We don't trust someone we don't know.

Learning the concepts of appropriate behavior and making them second nature to you will free you to interact with confidence and assurance and allow you to focus on the other person and the business at hand.

Brand management also demands consistency. People who know you learn to expect certain behaviors from you, and when you deviate dramatically from those behaviors, you need to be aware of the inconsistency and prepared to explain it. No one likes to work with the person who one day shows up as a great guy and the next day is replaced by his evil twin. Of course, we can't maintain total control all the time, but when you are self-aware, you can make sure your behavior remains professional and within reasonable boundaries of what people anticipate.

COMMITTING TO ONGOING LEARNING

A personal brand, although consistent, isn't static. As you grow and progress, you will need to continue modifying and amplifying aspects of your brand that are appropriate to the changes in your life and career. Many successful people understand that a secret to remaining relevant and vital, even into advanced years, hinges on a commitment to lifelong learning. We all know people who are old at forty—they've been there, and done that, and they don't have much desire to learn anything new. On the other hand, people in their seventies and eighties and beyond continue to make a difference in their organizations and in the world. Even though the essence of your personal brand will be the same whether you are thirty or fifty, the way that you exhibit it will mature along with you. You may add more to your repertoire. A former neighbor of mine who now lives in another city was a renowned jeweler and is now pursuing a career in oil painting in his late seventies. Continuing to learn new knowledge, skills, and abilities will enhance your brand throughout your career and life.

Establishing and maintaining a strong personal brand take effort, but the benefits are significant. Susan Chritton in *Personal Branding for Dummies* mentions increasing your confidence and differentiating yourself from the competition. Furthermore, the focus that self-branding requires will transfer to other areas of your career. And the ongoing self-knowledge will allow you to interact more effectively and productively with those around you.

THE BOTTOM LINE

➤ If you don't decide how you want others to perceive you, they will create their own perceptions.

➤ Your personal brand must be authentic and consistent.

➤ You will continue to modify and develop your brand throughout your life.

➤ A strong personal brand benefits you and allows you to be more effective with others.

A Final Word

*A*ll this talk about courtesy, sensitivity, and good behavior! Is it really necessary to "go by the book" in all the situations that we've explored?

Actually, the major purpose of the "how tos" of handling various situations is to get you thinking innovatively and wisely about how to treat other people in good times, bad times, and stressful, confusing times.

Focus on the ideas presented here that work for you and make a habit of applying them. You will be ahead of the game in the way you present yourself to the many different people with whom you interact daily, monthly, annually, or even those you encounter only once. If a particular chapter hits home or presents potential for your development, writing down your intentions or goals will help you achieve them faster.

As you may already be aware, courtesy and respect create a domino effect. Your behavior won't just benefit the people you treat well; those people will most likely remember your kindness the next time they are on the opposite end of a similar situation and behave accordingly. Your act of courtesy may prompt the receiver of that act to "pass it on." Eventually, we might all discover that being courteous is more rewarding and less taxing than being rude.

Rules of courtesy aren't intended to make you pompous or uptight. Indeed, they grew out of society's need to make the world a fairer, kinder, more comfortable place to live. Be ingenious and innovative in the way you apply the rules to your own circumstances. As one practice becomes irrelevant or outdated, come up with a version that meets current needs but keeps alive the essential spirit of the principle. Ulti-mately, all the guidelines on how to behave properly in any social situation come down to a simple principle: Treat others in a manner that values everyone and denigrates no one.

Becoming the person who can handle any situation with grace and confidence will get you noticed for the right reasons. And once the spotlight is on you, you can leverage your intelligence, your training, and your creativity to help you achieve your goals.

Acknowledgments

*T*he way that we interact with each other has been a subject of fascination for centuries, and this book is just one more look at particular facets of the process. In thinking and writing about the topic of workplace civility and the role of courtesy in personal success, I have been fortunate to benefit from the great accumulation of others' ideas and writings as a foundation for my own conclusions.

Further, in writing this book, I often called on colleagues, clients, students, friends, and family to discuss various concepts and, particularly, to share their own thoughts and experiences. I am grateful to all of them for their willingness to participate and add value.

Special thanks go to my husband, Charles Boyd, whose business experience and organized thought processes helped me focus and manage the seemingly unlimited information on the subject.

To all of you who contributed support, encouragement, and wisdom to this endeavor, I hope you will conclude that it was time well spent.

Bibliography

INTRODUCTION: THE CASE FOR COURTESY

Andersson, L., and C. Pearson. "Tit-for-Tat? The Spiraling Effect of Incivility in the Workplace." *Academy of Management Review* 24, no. 3 (July 1999): 452–471. www.sc.edu/ombuds/doc/Andersson_and_Pearson_1999.pdf.

Ivy Sea Online Leadership Communication Center. *Personal Mastery Series: What's Your Civility Quotient?* Last accessed February 21, 2016. www.ivysea.com/pages/ct0499_1.html.

Pearson, C. "Organizations as Targets and Triggers of Aggression and Violence." *Research in the Sociology of Organizations* 15 (1998): 197–223.

Pearson, C., L. Andersson, and C. Porath. "Assessing and Attacking Workplace Incivility." *Organizational Dynamics* (Fall 2000): 123–137.

Pearson, C., L. Andersson, and J. Wegner. "When Workers Flout Convention: A Preliminary Study of Workplace Incivility." *Human Relations* 54 (2001): 1387–1419.

Roche, Eileen. "Do Something—He's About to Snap." *Harvard Business Review*, July 2003, 23–31. hbr.org/2003/07/do-something-hes-about-to-snap.

PART 1: EVERYDAY COURTESY AS A SUCCESS FACTOR

Chapter 1: Manners in the Twenty-First Century

Caldwell, Mark. *A Short History of Rudeness: Manners, Morals, and Misbehavior in Modern America.* New York: First Picador, 2000.

Casperson, Dana May. *Power Etiquette: What You Don't Know Can Kill Your Career.* New York: AMACOM, 1999.

Craig, Elizabeth. *Don't Slurp Your Soup: A Basic Guide to Business Etiquette*, 2nd ed. St. Paul, MN: Brighton Publications, 1996.

Farkas, S., J. Johnson, A. Duffet, and K. Collins. "Aggravating Circumstances: A Status Report on Rudeness in America." New York: Public Agenda, 2002. www.publicagenda.org/files/aggravating_circumstances.pdf.

Jensen, Jaclyn M., Pankaj C. Patel, and Jana L. Raver. "Better to Be Average? High and Low Performance as Predictors of Employee Victimization." *Journal of Applied Psychology*, Vol 99(2), Mar 2014, 296-39. dx.doi. org/10.1037/a0034822

Ivy Sea Online Leadership Communication Center. *Personal Mastery Series: What Is Your Civility Quotient.* Last modified 2006. www.ivysea.com/pages/ct0499_1.html.

Porath, C., and C. Pearson. "The Price of Incivility." *Harvard Business Review*, January–February 2013.

Chapter 2: Credibility: Creating It and Keeping It

Booher, Dianna. *Creating Personal Presence.* San Francisco: Barrett-Koehler Publishers, 2011.

Lutz, William. *Double Speak.* New York: Harper Collins, 1990. First published 1981 by Harper Perennial.

———. *The New Doublespeak: Why No One Knows What Anyone's Saying Anymore.* New York: HarperCollins Publishers, 1996.

MacMillan, Pat. *The Performance Factor: Unlocking the Secrets of Teamwork.* Nashville: Broadman & Holman, 2001.

Pfeffer, Jeffrey, and Robert I Sutton. *The Knowing–Doing Gap: How Smart Companies Turn Knowledge into Action.* Boston: Harvard Business Press, 2000.

Chapter 3: Develop Your Gratitude Attitude: Say "Thank You" and Mean It

Post, Peggy, Peter Post, Lizzie Post, and Daniel Post Senning. *The Etiquette Advantage in Business, Third Edition: Personal Skills for Professional Success.* New York: Harper Collins Publishers, 2014.

Chapter 4: Are Your Nonverbal Messages Telling on You?

Booher, Dianna. *Creating Personal Presence.* San Francisco: Barrett-Koehler Publishers, 2011.

Elgin, Suzette Haden. *The Gentle Art of Verbal Self-Defense at Work.* Paramus, NJ: Prentice-Hall, 2000.

Goman, Carol Kinsey. *The Silent Language of Leaders: How Body Language Can Help—or Hurt—How You Lead.* San Francisco: Jossey-Bass, 2011.

Mole, John. *Mind Your Manners: Managing Business Cultures in the New Global Europe.* Yarmouth, ME: Nicholas Brealey Publishing, 2003.

Timm, Paul R. *Managerial Communication—A Finger on the Pulse*. Upper Saddle River, NJ: Prentice-Hall, 1995.

Chapter 5: What the $%#*!& Is Going On Here?

White, Carol. "The Increased Use of Slang and Profanity." Survey of students and faculty at Robinson College of Business, Georgia State University, Atlanta, 1999.

Chapter 7: Giving *Genuine* Compliments that Count

Booher, Dianna. *Communicate with Confidence*. Rev. ed. New York: McGraw-Hill, 2011.

Chapter 8: Improving Your Listening Skills

Booher, Dianna. *Communicate with Confidence*. Rev. ed. New York: McGraw-Hill, 2011.

Harkins, Phil. *Powerful Conversations: How High Impact Leaders Communicate*. New York: McGraw-Hill, 1999.

———. *Summary: Powerful Conversations: How High Impact Leaders Communicate*. BusinessNews Publishing, 2014. Kindle edition.

Isaacs, William. *Dialogue: The Art of Thinking Together*. New York: Currency, 1999.

———. *Dialogue: The Art of Thinking Together*. New York: Random House, 2008. Kindle edition.

McKay, Matthew, Martha Davis, and Patrick Fanning. *Messages: The Communication Skills Book*, 2nd ed. Oakland, CA: New Harbinger Publications, 2009.

Rankin, Paul R. "The Importance of Listening Ability". *The English Journal*, Vol. 17, No. 8 (Oct., 1928), pp. 623-630.

Chapter 9: Being Smart About Smartphones and Other Devices

Holmes, Dana. "A Much Needed Guide for Text Etiquette." *The Huffington Post*. Last updated March 17, 2013. www.huffingtonpost.com/dana-holmes/text-etiquette-guide_b_2474980.html

Petronzio, Matt. "U.S. Adults Spend 11 Hours Per Day With Digital Media." *Mashable*. March 5, 2014. http://mashable.com/2014/03/05/american-digital-media-hours/.

Chapter 10: Using Social Media to Make—Not Break—Your Career

Armstrong, Mario, and Janet Taylor. "Do's and don'ts of posting photos on social media." *TODAY Show.* Aired March 31, 2014. www.today.com/popculture/dos-donts-posting-photos-social-media-2D79455475.

Frankel, Lois. *Nice Girls Don't Get the Corner Office.* New York: Business Plus, 2014.

Loughman, Alison. "6 Social Media Mistakes You Might be Making." *Little Pink Book* (blog). August 8, 2014. www.littlepinkbook.com/6-social-media-mistakes-you-might-be-making/.

Chapter 11: Travel Courtesy: Don't Leave Home Without It

Caldwell, Mark. *A Short History of Rudeness: Manners, Morals, and Misbehavior in Modern America.* New York: Picador USA, 2000.

Morrison, Terri, Wayne Conaway, and George Borden. *Kiss, Bow, or Shake Hands: How to Do Business in Sixty Countries.* 2nd ed. Avon, MA: Adams Media, 2006.

Reif, Joe, Nargess Shahmanesh, Minoru Kosaka, and Sibylla Putzi. *The Global Road Warrior: 85 Country Handbook for the International Business Traveler.* San Rafael, CA: World Trade Press, 1998.

Teison, Herbert, and Nancy Dunnan. *Travel Smarts.* 2nd ed. Old Saybrook, CT: Globe Pequot Press, 1997.

PART 2: BEST BEHAVIORS AT WORK: INTERACTING WITH BOSSES AND PEERS

Chapter 12: Terror on Both Sides of the Desk: Relieving Interview Stress

Imundo, Louis. *Effective Supervisor's Handbook* 2nd edition. New York, NY: AMACOM, 1993.

MacMillan, Pat. *Hiring Excellence: Six Steps to Making Good People Decisions.* Colorado Springs, CO: Navpress, 1992.

Waldrop, Dawn E. *Best Impressions: How to Gain Professionalism, Promotion, and Profit.* Cleveland: Book Masters, 2000.

Chapter 13: The New Job: Getting Started on the Right Foot

Nelson, Bob. *1001 Ways to Take Initiative at Work*. New York: Workman Publishing Company, 1999.

Rozakis, Laurie, and Bob Rozakis. *The Complete Idiot's Guide to Office Politics*. New York: Alpha Books, 1998.

Chapter 15: Getting Along with Your Manager: Spotting and Solving Personality Problems

Post, Peggy, Peter Post, Lizzie Post, and Daniel Post Senning. *The Etiquette Advantage in Business, Third Edition: Personal Skills for Professional Success*. New York: Harper Collins Publishers, 2014.

Weinstein, Bob. I Hate *My Boss!* New York: McGraw Hill, 1998.

Chapter 16: How to Speak So Your Boss Will Listen

Tannen, Deborah, "The Power of Talk: Who Gets Heard and Why." *Harvard Business Review*, September-October, 1995.

Chapter 17: E-mail: Think Before You Send

Casperson, Dana May. *Power Etiquette: What You Don't Know Can Kill Your Career*. New York: AMACOM, 1999.

McGinty, Sarah Myers. *Power Talk: Using Language to Build Authority and Influence*. New York: Warner Business Books, 2001.

Radicati Group. *The Email Statistics Report, 2011–2015*. Edited by Sara Radicati. Principal Analyst, Quoc Hoang. Palo Alto, CA: Radicati Group. May 2011. www.radicati.com/wp/wp-content/uploads/2011/05/Email-Statistics-Report-2011-2015-Executive-Summary.pdf.

Chapter 19: Dress Code Confusion

Waldrop, Dawn E. *Best Impressions: How to Gain Professionalism and Profit*. Cleveland: Book Masters, 2000.

Williams, David. "First Impressions Count: The Business Value of Dressing for Success," *Forbes*. August 9, 2013. www.forbes.com/sites/davidkwilliams/2013/08/09/first-impressions-count-the-business-value-of-dressing-for-success/.

Chapter 20: Mastering the Art of Meetings

Langford, Beverly Y. "Mastering the Art of Meetings," *Womentics*, August 2009.

Pittampalli, Al. *Read This Before Our Next Meeting: The Modern Meeting Standard*. Domino Project, 2011.

Triaxia Partners, Inc. "High Performance Meetings." Workshop, 1997, 2003.

Chapter 21: When Meetings Go Virtual

Bisharat, Jaleh. "8 Tips for Running a Virtual Meeting Like a Rockstar." *Huffington Post*. December 12, 2013; updated February 11, 2014. www. huffingtonpost.com/jaleh-bisharat/8-tips-for-running-a-virtual-meeting_b_44thirty375.html.

Chapter 22: How to Leave a Job: Making a Graceful Exit

Cantore, Jean Ann. "How to Quit Your Job Gracefully." *High Technology Careers*, October/November 1993, p. 34.

Chapter 23: Refuse to Schmooze and You Lose: Cultivating the Social Side of Business

Mandell, Terri. *Power Schmoozing: The New Etiquette for Social and Business Success*. New York: McGraw-Hill, 1996.

Naisbitt, John. *Megatrends: Ten New Directions Transforming Our Lives*. New York: Warner Books, 1986.

Chapter 24: Let's Do Lunch: Dining Your Way to Success

Post, Peggy, Peter Post, Lizzie, Post, and Daniel Post Senning. *The Etiquette Advantage in Business, Third Edition: Personal Skills for Professional Success*. New York: Harper Collins Publishers, 2014.

Chapter 25: Getting Noticed—Without Becoming Notorious

Kelley, Robert E. *How to Be a Star at Work*. New York: Times Books, 1998.

Mosvick, Roger K., and Robert B. Nelson. *We've Got to Start Meeting Like This*. 2nd ed. New York: Park Avenue Productions, 1996.

Nelson, Bob. *1001 Ways to Take Initiative at Work*. New York: Workman Publishing Company, 1999.

Chapter 26: He Said, She Said: When the Gender Gap Seems as Wide as the Grand Canyon

Kyung Kim, Eun. "Chatty Cathy, listen up: New study reveals why women talk more than men." *TODAY Health*, February 21, 2013. www.today.com/health/chatty-cathy-listen-new-study-reveals-why-women-talk-more-1C8469360.

MacRae, Fiona. "Women talk three times as much as men, says study." *Daily Mail*. November 28, 2006. www.dailymail.co.uk/femail/article-4190forty/Women-talk-times-men-says-study.html.

McGinty, Sarah Myers. *Power Talk: Using Language to Build Authority and Influence*. New York: Warner Business Books, 2001.

Rozakis, Laurie, and Bob Rozakis, *The Complete Idiot's Guide to Office Politics*. New York: Alpha Books, 1998.

Tannen, Deborah. *Talking from 9 to 5: Women and Men in the Workplace*. New York: Avon Books, 1995.

———. *You Just Don't Understand: Women and Men in Conversation*. New York: Harper Collins, 2007.

Thomas, Jane. *Guide to Managerial Persuasion and Influence*. Prentice Hall Series in Advanced Business Communication. Upper Saddle River, NJ: Prentice Hall, 2003.

Tymson, Candy. *Gender Games: Doing Business with the Opposite Sex*. Sydney: Tymson Communications, 1998. www.tymson.com.au/articles.html.

Chapter 27: Citizenship in the Global Village

Chaney, Lillian H., and Jeanette S. Martin. *Intercultural Business Communication*. 2nd ed. Upper Saddle River, NJ: Prentice-Hall, 2000.

Kenton, Sherron Bienvenu, and Deborah Valentine. *Crosstalk: Communicating in a Multicultural Workplace*. Upper Saddle River, NJ: Prentice-Hall, 1997.

Morrison, Terri, Wayne Conaway, and George Borden. *Kiss, Bow, or Shake Hands: How to Do Business in Sixty Countries*. 2nd ed. Avon, MA: Adams Media, 2006.

Penrose, John M., Robert W. Rasberry, and Robert J. Myers. *Business Communication for Managers: An Advanced Approach*. Mason, OH: Thomson South-Western, 2004.

Thiederman, Sondra. *Profiting in America's Multicultural Marketplace:*

How to Do Business Across Cultural Lines. New York: Lexington Books, 1991.

PART 3: HANDLING SENSITIVE ISSUES: COURTESY AND BUILDING TRUST

Chapter 30: Dealing With A Bully Boss

Annunzio, Susan, "Are You a Workplace Bully?" *Inc.com.* Last accessed January 22, 2014. www.inc.com/the-build-network/are-you-a-work-place-bully-take-this-test-to-find-out.html,

Horn, Sam, *Take the Bully by the Horns: Stop Unethical, Uncooperative or Unpleasant People from Running and Ruining your Life.* New York: St. Martin's Press, 2002.

McDonald, Jay. "Is an Office Bully Ruining your Job?" *Bankrate.com.* Last accessed August 6, 2004. http://www.bankrate.com/brm/news/advice/20011102a.asp

———. "Beating a Bullying Boss," *Bankrate.com.* Last accessed August 17, 2004. http://www.bankrate.com/finance/jobs-careers/beating-a-bullying-boss.aspx

Morrill, Calvin, as quoted in *New York Times* "Learning Network: Teacher Connection – Fear in the Workplace: The Bullying Boss," by Benedict Carey, June 22, 2004.

Namie, Gary. The Workplace Bullying Institute. Last Accessed February 22, 2016. www.workplacebullying.org/the-drs-namie/

Chapter 31: Dealing with Negative Coworkers

Amabile, Teresa. "Brilliant but Cruel: Perceptions of Negative Evaluators." *Journal of Experimental Social Psychology* 19, no. 2 (March 1983): 146–156.

Heathfield, Susan. "The Five Causes of Employee Negativity." *About Money.* Updated June 14, 2015. http://humanresources.about.com/od/workrelationships/ a/negativitycause.htm.

Pfeffer, Jeffrey, and Sutton , Robert I. *The Knowing–Doing Gap: How Smart Companies Turn Knowledge into Action.* Boston: Harvard Business School Press, 2000.

Vulcan, Nicole. "Tips on Dealing with Negative Co-workers." *eHow* www.ehow.com/how_2162073.

Chapter 33: An Apology Is in Order: Repairing the Damage with a Sincere Response

Booher, Dianna. *Communicate with Confidence.* New York: McGraw-Hill, 1994.

Tannen, Deborah. *Talking from 9 to 5: Women and Men in the Workplace.* New York: Avon Books, 1995.

Chapter 34: Delivering Unwelcome Information Without Damaging Relationships

Booher, Dianna. *Communicate with Confidence.* New York: McGraw-Hill, 2011

Chapter 35: Confronting with Courtesy: Preserving Relationships While Resolving Differences

"From Strife to Synergy," a workshop developed by Team Resources, Inc., 1988, 2000.

Katzenbach, Jon R. and Douglas K. Smith. *The Wisdom of Teams: Creating the High-Performance Organization.* Boston: Collins Business Essentials, 2003.

Pickering, Peg. *How to Manage Conflict: Turn All Conflicts into Win-Win Outcomes.* 3rd ed. Franklin Lakes, NJ: Career Press, 2000.

Chapter 36: When the Worst Happens: Dealing with Tragedy, Illness, and Death

Emel, Bobbi. "7 Things to Say (and Not Say) to a Grieving Person." *Lifehack.* www.lifehack.org/articles/communication/7-things-to-say-and-not-say- to-a-grieving-person.html.

Sherwood, Glynis. "How to Talk to Grieving People: 4 Essential Guidelines." *Glynis Sherwood Counselling* (blog). November 28, 2011. www.glynissherwood.com/blog/how-to-talk-to-grieving-people-nov-28-2011-6-56-29-am-29.

Chapter 37: Putting It All Together: Creating and Maintaining Your Personal Brand

Arruda, William. "3 Critical Questions to Ask Yourself Before Building Your Personal Brand," *Forbes.* March 11, 2014. www.forbes.com/sites/

williamarruda/2014/03/11/3-critical-questions-to-ask-yourself-before-building-your-personal-brand/.

Bates, Suzanne "The Science of Influence: The Three Dimensions of Executive Presence." Bates Communications, www.bates-communications.com/articles-and-newsletters/articles-and-newsletters/bid/579thirty/The-Science-of-Influence-The-Three-Dimensions-of-Executive-Presence.

Chritton, Susan. "Ten Key Benefits of Personal Branding." *Personal Branding for Dummies.* Hoboken, NJ: Wiley, 2012. www.dummies.com/how-to/content/ten-key-benefits-of-personal-branding.html.

Harrison, Craig. "Sample Elevator Speeches." *Expressions of Excellence.* www.expressionsofexcellence.com/sample_elevator.html.

Harry, Sean. "What's a Personal Brand and Why Do You Need One?" *CAREERALISM.* March 20, 2013. www.careerealism.com/personal-brand/.

Peters, Tom. "The Brand Called You." *Fast Company.* August 31, 1997. www.fastcompany.com/28905/brand-called-you.

Reinhold, Barbara. "Build Your Brand." *Monster.com.* http://career-advice.monster.com/job-search/professional-networking/build-your-brand/article.aspx.

Westfall, Chris. *The New Elevator Pitch.* Dallas: Marie Street Press, 2012.

Index

About the Author

*B*everly Y. Langford, PhD, is President of LMA Communication, a consulting, training, and coaching firm that works with organizations and individuals on strategic communication, message development, effective interpersonal communication skills, team building, and leadership development. She has designed numerous courses in these areas and works closely with companies to tailor training on a variety of subjects to the organizations' specific requirements. In addition, Dr. Langford teaches strategic communication to graduate students at Georgia State University's Robinson College of Business. She is a member of the Association of Business Communicators and the Association of Professional Communication Consultants. She received a BA degree from the University of Mississippi, an MA from Memphis State University (now the University of Memphis), and a PhD from Georgia State University.